Critters & Company

Pam Schiller

Special Needs Adaptations by Clarissa Willis

Acknowledgments

I would like to thank the following people for their contributions to this book. The special needs adaptations were written by Clarissa Willis. The

Clarissa Willis   Patrick Brennan   Richele Bartkowiak

CD is arranged by Patrick Brennan, and performed by Richele Bartkowiak and Patrick Brennan. It was engineered and mixed by Jeff Smith at Southwest Recordings. —Pam Schiller

Books written by Pam Schiller

The Bilingual Book of Rhymes, Songs, Stories, and Fingerplays, with Rafael Lara-Alecio and Beverly J. Irby

The Complete Book of Activities, Games, Stories, Props, Recipes, and Dances, with Jackie Silberg

The Complete Book of Rhymes, Songs, Poems, Fingerplays, and Chants, with Jackie Silberg

The Complete Daily Curriculum for Early Childhood: Over 1200 Easy Activities to Support Multiple Intelligences and Learning Styles, with Pat Phipps

The Complete Resource Book: An Early Childhood Curriculum, with Kay Hastings

The Complete Resource Book for Infants: Over 700 Experiences for Children From Birth to 18 Months

The Complete Resource Book for Toddlers and Twos: Over 2000 Experiences and Ideas

Count on Math: Activities for Small Hands and Lively Minds, with Lynne Peterson

Creating Readers: Over 1000 Games, Activities, Tongue Twisters, Fingerplays, Songs, and Stories to Get Children Excited About Reading

Do You Know the Muffin Man?, with Thomas Moore

The Instant Curriculum, Revised, with Joan Rosanno

The Practical Guide to Quality Child Care, with Patricia Carter Dyke

Start Smart: Building Brain Power in the Early Years

The Values Book, with Tamera Bryant

Where Is Thumbkin?, with Thomas Moore

CD INSIDE!

CRITTERS & COMPANY

Pam Schiller

Gryphon House, Inc.
Beltsville, Maryland

Bulk purchase

Gryphon House books are available for special premiums and sales promotions as well as for fund-raising use. Special editions or book excerpts also can be created to specification. For details, contact the Marketing Director at Gryphon House.

Critters & Company

© 2006 Pam Schiller
Printed in the United States of America.

Illustrations: Deborah Johnson
Cover Photograph: Getty Images, ©2005.

Published by Gryphon House, Inc.
10726 Tucker Street, Beltsville, MD 20705
301.595.9500; 301.595.0051 (fax); 800.638.0928 (toll-free)

Visit us on the web at www.ghbooks.com

 Gryphon House is a member of the Green Press Initiative, a nonprofit program dedicated to supporting publishers in their efforts to reduce their use of fiber sourced forests. For further information visit www.greenpressinitiative.org

Library of Congress Cataloging-in-Publication Data

Schiller, Pamela Byrne.
  Critters and company / Pam Schiller ; illustrations, Deborah Johnson.
     p. cm.
  Includes bibliographical references and index.
    ISBN-13: 978-0-87659-017-1
  ISBN-10: 0-87659-017-2
  1. Preschool music--Instruction and study--Activity programs. 2. Music in education. 3. Children's songs, English--Texts. 4. Animals--Songs and music. I. Title.
    MT920.S38 2006
    372.8'704--dc22

                                              2006007623

Table of Contents

Before serving food to children, be aware of children's food allergies and sensitivities, as well as any religious or cultural practices that exclude certain foods. Be sure to incorporate this information into your daily planning.

Introduction

Music in the Early Years

Music is a universal language, and singing is a hallmark of the early childhood classroom. Children love to sing! Teachers love to sing! Age makes no difference. Culture makes no difference.

Singing songs enriches thematic content, supports literacy concepts, and optimizes memory and learning. Add extensions of classroom activities, including modifications for special needs and English language learner populations, and it's a perfect package. *Critters and Company* is one of eight thematic CD/book sets that offer all of these resources in one package.

Thematic Content

Critters and Company overlaps several typical early childhood themes: Animals, Zoo, Farm, Pets, Traditional Tales and Imagination. Read the lyrics and then decide the best fit for each song in your curriculum.

Each song is accompanied by a list of facts titled "Did You Know?" These facts provide background information about the song, interesting facts about the topic or lyrics, historical information, or some form of trivia you might use as a springboard to discussion. This feature will save you hours of research and adds significantly to the value of the song.

Literacy Concepts

Preschool children need experiences that allow them to develop and practice basic literacy skills: listening, oral language development, phonological awareness, letter knowledge, print awareness, and comprehension. Suggestions for using the songs on *Critters and Company* as a springboard for teaching these literacy skills accompany every title. Below is a definition for each literacy skill and the sub-skills they encompass.

○ **Listening:** the development of age-appropriate attention span, as well as the ability to listen for a variety of purposes; for example, details, directions, and sounds.

○ **Oral Language Development:** the acquisition of vocabulary, the fine-tuning of grammar, and the increase in sentence length and complexity.

o **Phonological Awareness:** sensitivity to the sounds of language. Phonological awareness begins with babbling and cooing and goes all the way through the understanding of sound and symbol relationships and decoding. The skills in the higher end of the phonological awareness continuum—sound and symbol relationship and decoding—are appropriate for children who are age five or older.

o **Segmentation:** the breaking apart of words by syllable or letter; for example, children clap the breaks in the word *di-no-saur.*

o **Rhyme:** words that sound alike. The ending sound of the words is the same, but the initial consonant sound is different, for example, *cat* and *hat* or *rake* and *cake.*

o **Alliteration:** the repetition of a consonant sound in a series of words; for example, Peter Piper picked a peck of pickled peppers. Children need to be able to hear the repetition of the /p/ sound, but do not need to identify that the sound is made by the letter "p".

o **Onomatopoeia:** words that imitate the sound they are describing; for example, *pitter-patter, moo, quack, beep,* and so on.

o **Letter Knowledge:** the visual recognition of each letter of the alphabet, both lowercase and uppercase.

o **Print Awareness:** the understanding that print has many functions; for example, telling a story, making a list, as part of signs, in news articles, in recipes, and so on. It is also the awareness that print moves left to right and top to bottom.

o **Comprehension:** the internalization of a story or a concept.

Optimizing Memory and Learning

Singing boosts memory and keeps the brain alert. Increased memory and alertness optimize the potential for learning. When we sing we generally feel good. That sense of well-being causes the brain to release endorphins into the blood stream and those endorphins act as a memory fixative. When we sing we automatically increase our oxygen intake, which, in turn, increases our alertness. Scientific research has validated what early childhood professionals know intuitively—that singing has a positive effect on learning.

Expanding Children's Learning With Activities

Using songs as a springboard for activities is a good way to bring the lyrics of the song into a meaningful context for children. Observing real ducks after singing "Six White Ducks" reinforces and creates meaningful context for the specific characteristics of this type of animal. Making a "bushy tail," examining acorns, discussing the life of a squirrel walking a "telephone line," after singing "Gray Squirrel" helps children better understand the characteristics of squirrels, as well as the role squirrels play in the environment.

Reading a book about seeds after singing about seeds also helps expand children's understanding. For that reason literature selections are provided for each song. Integrating the teaching of themes and skills with songs, literature, and multidisciplinary activities provides a comprehensive approach for helping children recognize the patterns and the interconnected relationships of what they are learning.

Throughout the book, questions to ask children appear in italics. These questions are intended to help children think and reflect on what they have learned. This reflective process optimizes the opportunity for children to apply the information and experiences they have encountered.

Modifications

Suggestions for children with special needs and suggestions for English language learners accompany the song activities when appropriate. These features allow teachers to use the activities with diverse populations. All children love to sing and the benefits apply to all!

Special Needs

The inclusion of children with disabilities in preschool and child care programs is increasingly common. Parents, teachers, and researchers have found that children benefit in many ways from integrated programs that are designed to meet the needs of all children. Many children with disabilities, however, need accommodations to participate successfully in the general classroom.

Included in the extensions and activities for each song are adaptations for children with special needs. These adaptations allow *all* children to experience the song and related activities in a way that will maximize their learning opportunities. The adaptations are specifically for children who have needs in the following areas:

○ sensory integration
○ distractibility
○ hearing loss
○ spatial organization
○ language, receptive and expressive
○ fine motor coordination
○ cognitive challenges

The following general strategies from Kathleen Bulloch (2003) are for children who have difficulty listening and speaking.

Difficulty	Adaptations/Modifications/Strategies
Listening	○ State the objective—provide a reason for listening ○ Use a photo card ○ Give explanations in small, discrete steps ○ Be concise with verbal information: "Evan, please sit," instead of "Evan, would you please sit down in your chair?" ○ Provide visuals ○ Have the child repeat directions ○ Have the child close his eyes and try to visualize the information ○ Provide manipulative tasks ○ When giving directions to the class, leave a pause between each step so the child can carry out the process in her mind ○ Shorten the listening time required ○ Pre-teach difficult vocabulary and concepts
Verbal Expression	○ Provide a prompt, such as beginning the sentence for the child or giving a picture cue ○ Accept an alternate form of information-sharing, such as artistic creation, photos, charade or pantomime, and demonstration ○ Ask questions that require short answers ○ Specifically teach body and language expression ○ First ask questions at the information level—giving facts and asking for facts back ○ Wait for children to respond; don't call on the first child to raise his hand ○ Have the child break in gradually by speaking in smaller groups and then in larger groups

English Language Learners

Strategies for English language learners are also provided to maximize their learning.

The following are general strategies for working with English language learners (Gray, Fleischman, 2004-05):

○ **Keep the language simple.** Speak simply and clearly. Use short, complete sentences in a normal tone of voice. Avoid using slang, idioms, or figures of speech.

○ **Use actions and illustrations to reinforce oral statements.** Appropriate prompts and facial expressions help convey meaning.

○ **Ask for completion, not generation.** Ask children to choose answers from a list or to complete a partially finished sentence. Encourage children to use language as much as possible, so they can gain confidence over time.

○ **Model correct usage and judiciously correct errors.** Use corrections to positively reinforce children's use of English. When English language learners make a mistake or use awkward language, they are often attempting to apply what they know about their first language to English. For example, a Spanish-speaking child may say, "It fell from me," a direct translation from Spanish, instead of "I dropped it."

○ **Use visual aids.** Present classroom content and information in a way that engages children—by using graphic organizers (word web, story maps), photographs, concrete materials, and graphs, for example.

Involving English Language Learners in Music Activities

Music is a universal language that draws people together. For English language learners, music can be a powerful vehicle for language learning and community-building. Music and singing are important to second language learners for many reasons, including:

○ The rhythms of music help children hear the sounds and intonation patterns of a new language.

○ Musical lyrics and accompanying motions help children learn new vocabulary.

○ Repetitive patterns of language in songs help children internalize the sentence structure of English.

○ Important cultural information is conveyed to young children in the themes of songs.

Strategies for involving English language learners in music activities vary according to the child's level of proficiency in the English language.

Level of Proficiency	Strategies
Beginning English Language Learners	o Keep the child near you and model motions as you engage in group singing. o Use hand gestures, movements, and signs as often as possible to accompany song lyrics, making sure to tie a specific motion to a specific word. o Refer to real objects in the environment that are named in a song. o Stress the intonation, sounds, and patterns in language by speaking the lyrics of the song while performing actions or referring to objects in the environment. o Use simple, more common vocabulary. For example, use *round* instead of *circular*.
Intermediate-Level English Language Learners	o Say the song before singing it, so children can hear the words and rhythms of the lyrics. o Use motions, gestures, and signs to help children internalize the meaning of song lyrics. Be sure the motion is tied clearly to the associated word. o Throughout the day, repeat the language patterns found in songs in various activities. o Stress the language patterns in songs, and pause as children fill in the blanks. o Adapt the patterns of song, using familiar vocabulary.
Advanced English Language Learners	o Use visuals to cue parts of a song. o Use graphic organizers to introduce unfamiliar information. o Use synonyms for words heard in songs to expand children's vocabulary. o Develop vocabulary through description and comparison. For example, it is *round* like a circle. It is *circular*. o Encourage children to make up new lyrics for songs.

How to Use This Book

Use the 27 songs on the *Critters and Company* CD (included with this book) and the related activities in the book to enhance themes in your curriculum, or use them independently. Either way you have a rich treasure chest of creative ideas for your classroom.

The eight package collection provides more than 200 songs, a perfect combination of traditional best-loved children's songs and brand-new selections created for each theme. Keep a song in your heart and put joy in your teaching!

Bibliography

Bulloch, K. 2003. *The mystery of modifying: Creative solutions.* Huntsville, TX: Education Service Center, Region VI.

Cavallaro, C. & M. Haney. 1999. *Preschool inclusion.* Baltimore, MD: Paul H. Brookes Publishing Company.

Gray, T. and S. Fleischman. Dec. 2004-Jan. 2005. "Research matters: Successful strategies for English language learners." *Educational Leadership,* 62, 84-85.

Hanniford, C. 1995. *Smart moves: Why learning is not all in your head.* Arlington, VA: Great Ocean Publications, p. 146.

LeDoux, J. 1993. "Emotional memory systems in the brain." *Behavioral and Brain Research,* 58.

Tabors, P. 1997. *One child, two languages: Children learning English as a second language.* Baltimore, MD: Paul H. Brookes Publishing Company.

Songs and Activities

One Elephant

One elephant went out to play
Out on a spider's web one day.
He had such enormous fun,
He called another elephant
    to come.

Two elephants went out to play
Out on a spider's web one day.
They had such enormous fun,
They called for another
    elephant to come.

Additional verses:
Three elephants went out
    to play…
Four elephants went out
    to play…
Five elephants went out to play…

Directions: Children sit in a circle. One child places one arm out in front to make a trunk, then walks around the circle while the group sings the song. When the group sings "called for another elephant to come," the first child chooses another child to become an "elephant." The first child extends her free hand between her legs to make a tail. The second child extends one arm to make a trunk and grabs hold of the first child's tail. The two walk trunk to tail as the song continues.

Vocabulary

elephant
enormous
spider
web

Theme Connections

Big and Little
Insects
Nursery Rhymes

Did You Know?

○ Elephants are the largest mammals in the world that live on land. They can live as long as eighty years!

○ Soft spongy pads on the soles of their feet absorb noise, allowing these massive beasts to move through the bush with very little commotion.

○ Elephants are plant-eaters. Because they are such big animals, they need to eat large amounts of leaves, grass, and tree bark. They spend as much as twenty hours a day eating! A full-grown African elephant can weigh more than 10,000 pounds!

○ The ears of a full-grown African elephant are about five to six feet long and four feet wide. Elephants sometimes flap their ears to cool themselves.

○ An elephant's trunk is part nose and part upper lip. An elephant breathes through its trunk. Elephants also smell and pick up things with it. They use it to put food into their mouths, and even spray water with it! An elephant's trunk can grow to be ten feet long.

○ Elephants communicate with each other by making sounds called "tummy rumbles." They also make a "trumpeting" sound to call to each other.

○ See page 107 for more information about elephants.

Literacy Links

Comprehension

○ Discuss elephants. Make a KWL chart as follows. Create three columns on a sheet of chart paper. Label the first column "What We Know," the second column, "What We Want to Know" and the last column "What We Learned." Under the first column list facts the children know about elephants. In the second column list what the children would like to know about elephants. After the children are finished talking about elephants, list the things they learned in the third column.

○ Change the words to the song. Sing, "One dinosaur went out to play, out on a mountainside one day." Ask the children where other animals might play, for example, one bumblebee (in a honeycomb), one little frog (on a lily pad), and so on.

○ Challenge the children to help create a Venn Diagram. Draw two large overlapping circles on chart paper. In one circle have the children dictate a list of all the things they know about spiders. In the second circle have the children dictate a list of all the things they know about elephants. Use the section in the middle created by the overlapping circles to list the things that are true about both spiders and elephants.

○ Teach the children "The Elephant."

The Elephant
The elephant goes
Like this, like that. (move around slowly on all fours)
He's terribly big, (stand up, reach arms high)
And he's terribly fat. (stretch arms out to the sides)
He has no fingers, (put hands in fists, hiding fingers)
He has no toes, (wiggle toes)
But goodness gracious,
What a nose! (put elbow to nose, as if extending trunk)

Letter Recognition

○ Print *elephant* on chart paper. Ask children to identify the letters. *Which letter appears twice?*

Oral Language

○ Discuss the weight of an elephant as it pertains to the strength of a spider's web. *Would the web hold the weight of an elephant?*

○ Discuss the meaning of *enormous*. Point out the cleverness of using the word enormous when it is used to describe the fun an elephant is having. Challenge the children to think of other words to substitute for *enormous*.

○ Teach the children the American Sign Language signs for *elephant* and *spider* (pages 121-123).

Phonological Awareness

○ Clap the syllables of *elephant*. Challenge the children to think of other animals with three-syllable names.

> ✓ **Special Needs Adaptation:** Invite the child to tap the syllables with a drum stick or pencil. For children with cognitive challenges, adapt the activity by naming other animals with three-syllable names. Then, together clap or tap the syllables of these animal names. You may need to prompt the child by counting with him, until he understands what you are asking him to do.

Curriculum Connections

Art

○ Make marble painting spider webs. Place a sheet of black construction paper in a shallow box. Place several marbles in a shallow cup of white tempera paint. Invite the children to place a paint-covered marble in the box and move the box around so that the marble rolls over the paper, creating a web effect.

Discovery

○ Wrap plastic wrap around a Styrofoam meat tray to create a wrinkle effect. Provide water and eyedroppers and invite the children to drop water onto the wrinkled surface. Tell the children that the elephant's wrinkled skin holds water, which helps keep the elephant cool.

○ Cut sponges into the shape of elephant feet and place them on a metal tray. Have the children stand over the tray and drop washers onto the sponges. Do the washers make more noise when they hit the sponge or the tray? Remind the children that elephants have spongy pads on their feet that help absorb the sounds that they make when they walk.

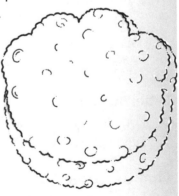

Gross Motor

○ Create a spider web with white yarn, winding the yarn around table legs, chair backs, doorknobs, and other things in the room. Encourage the children to crawl through the web without touching the yarn.

Language

○ Provide photos of large things, such as trees, hills, horses, and boats, and really large things, such as mountains, giant sequoias, dinosaurs, and ocean liners. Challenge the children to sort the photos into large things and enormous things.

Math

○ Use masking tape to outline the shape of an elephant's ear on the floor. The ears of a full-grown African elephant are about six feet long and four feet wide. Help the children see how many children can fit inside an elephant's ear.

○ Give children a 10" long strip of white poster board to represent the length of an elephant's tooth. Have the children find things in the room that are also 10" long.

Special Needs Adaptation: Adapt this activity by walking around the room with the child and helping her measure items that you point out to her. Model for her how to place her poster board elephant tooth against an item to determine if the item is the same size. Verbalize the results. Hearing you say out loud, "Look, the shelf is the same size as your pretend elephant's tooth," will reinforce the idea that you are comparing the object to the poster board.

Outdoors

○ Provide a ten foot piece of rope. Remind the children that the rope is the same length as a mature elephant's trunk. Encourage the children to use the rope to play Pull the Elephant's Trunk as you would play Tug of War.

Snack

○ Have the children wash their hands. Thoroughly mix ½ cup peanut butter, ½ cup honey, and 1 cup nonfat powdered milk. Squeeze and pull until the dough is shiny and soft. Roll into balls. Make some balls about the size of ping-pong balls and some balls the size of marbles. Chill. Place the balls, red licorice laces, and cinnamon candies on the table. Invite the children to follow the Friendly Spider Rebus Recipe (page 110) to make friendly spiders for snack. **Allergy Warning:** Check for peanut allergies.

Home Connection

○ Encourage families to hunt for spider webs outside their homes.

Book Corner

The Ant and the Elephant by Bill Peet

The Elephant's Pillow by Diana Reynolds Roome

One Little Elephant by Colin West

The Saggy Baggy Elephant by Kathryn Jackson

"Stand Back," Said the Elephant, "I'm Going to Sneeze" by Patricia Thomas

El Señor Don Gato

Oh, Señor Don Gato was a cat.
On a high red roof Don Gato sat.
He went there to read a letter,
Meow, meow, meow.
Where the reading light
   was better,
Meow, meow, meow.
'Twas a love note for Don Gato.

"I adore you," wrote the lady cat,
Who was fluffy, white and nice
   and fat.
There was not a sweeter kitty,
Meow, meow, meow,
In the country or the city,
Meow, meow, meow.
And she said she'd wed
   Don Gato.

Oh, Don Gato jumped so happily,
He fell off the roof and broke his
   knee.
Broke his ribs and all his whiskers,
Meow, meow, meow,
And his little solar plexus,
Meow, meow, meow.
"Ay caramba!" cried Don Gato.

Then the doctors all came on the
   run
Just to see if something could
   be done.
And they held a consultation,
Meow, meow, meow,
About how to save their patient,
Meow, meow, meow.
How to save Señor Don Gato.

But in spite of everything
   they tried

Poor Señor Don Gato up
   and died.
And it wasn't very merry,
Meow, meow, meow,
Going to the cemetery,
Meow, meow, meow,
For the ending of Don Gato.

When the funeral passed the
   market square,
Such a smell of fish was in the air.
Though his burial was slated,
Meow, meow, meow,
He became reanimated,
Meow, meow, meow.
He came back to life, Don Gato.

Olé!

Special Needs Adaptation: For children with special needs who have difficulty controlling their movements, use this song as an opportunity to talk about being kind to animals and using a gentle touch when handling them. Also, talk about how a cat might protect herself, such as using her claws. Show a picture of a cat that is hissing or getting ready to swat at something. Explain that this is what a cat does when she is upset. Also talk about animal safety, such as never touching an animal that is trying to eat or asking the owner's permission before touching a strange cat or dog.

Vocabulary

broke
burial
cemetery
city
consultation
county
doctor
fluffy
funeral
gato
knee
love letter
market
meow
olé
patient
reanimated
ribs
roof
Señor
slated
solar plexus
whiskers

Theme Connections

Community Workers
Make-Believe
Traditional Tales

Did You Know?

○ "El Señor Don Gato" is a popular traditional Latin song.

○ Both domestic and wild cats have intrigued humans for thousands of years; cats have been symbols of beauty, grace, mystery, and power.

○ Today, the domestic cat (house cat) is second only to the dog in popularity as a pet. Researchers estimate that there are more than 30 million pet cats.

○ Cats use their whiskers as "feelers" to determine if a space is wide enough for them to pass through.

○ See page 107 for more information about cats.

Literacy Links

Comprehension

○ Print *cat* in the middle of a sheet of chart paper. Draw a circle around the word. Ask children to tell you things they know about cats. Print their information on lines that extend outward from the circled word.

Oral Language

○ Point out the Spanish words in the song.

○ Teach the children the American Sign Language signs for *cat* and *I love you* (pages 121-122).

Phonological Awareness

○ Encourage the children to brainstorm a list of words that rhyme with cat.

○ Discuss the sounds Don Gato makes—"meow, meow, meow." Explain that words that imitate the sound they are describing are called *onomatopoeic* words. *Are there any other onomatopoeic words in the song?*

Curriculum Connections

Art

○ Show children how to draw a cat by drawing a smaller circle on top of a larger circle to make a cat's head. Add ears, eyes, and whiskers to the small circle and draw a tail attached to the larger circle.

Construction

○ Provide a 6" paper plate and an eight-inch paper plate, glue, tempera paint, markers, chenille stems, construction paper, and wiggle eyes. Encourage the children to glue the small plate

Book Corner

to the larger plate to create a cat. Encourage them to paint their cats and add construction paper ears and a tail. Have them use the markers for facial features, toothpicks for whiskers, and wiggle eyes for eyes.

Dramatic Play

❍ Provide a stethoscope, bandages, a toy cat, and other materials for a veterinary clinic. Invite the children to nurse Don Gato back to health.

Games

❍ Teach the children how to play "Old Gray Cat" (page 106).

Gross Motor

❍ Make a tunnel from medium-sized cardboard boxes (no wider than 16"). Make a cat mask from a paper plate. Cut whiskers from construction paper and glue them onto the mask. Have the whiskers extend two inches past the edge of the plate. Encourage the children to wear the masks as they crawl through the tunnel. *Do the whiskers touch the side of the box?*

Language

❍ Give the children the Animal Rhyming Word Cards (page 120). Encourage them to find the words that rhyme with *cat*.

Science

❍ Provide x-rays and pictures of bones for the children to observe. Discuss the bones we have in our bodies. Explain that our bones enable us to hold our bodies up.

Writing

❍ Print *cat* on chart paper. Invite the children to use magnetic letters to copy the word.
❍ Provide envelopes, paper, stamps, and other related materials. Encourage children to write love letters (or draw love letters) to their families.

Home Connection

❍ Encourage the children to talk to their families. Did any parents have pet cats when they were children?

Bingo

Vocabulary

dog
farmer
name

Theme Connections

Farms
Pets

There was a farmer had a dog,
And Bingo was his name-o.
B-I-N-G-O,
B-I-N-G-O,
B-I-N-G-O,
And Bingo was his name-o.

(Repeat, each time clapping to replace the next letter until the dog's name is clapped entirely.)

Did You Know?
○ Dogs are one of the most popular pets in the world.
○ Dogs were one of the first animals domesticated by humans. Dogs have been domesticated for most of human history and have endeared themselves to us. Stories have been told about brave dogs that served admirably in war or that risked their lives to save people in danger.
○ The smallest mature dog was a Yorkshire Terrier that was 2 ½ inches high at its shoulder. The heaviest dog ever weighed 319 pounds. The oldest dog ever died at age 29. The tallest dog ever was a Great Dane that stood 41 inches high.
○ The first living creature sent into space, a female dog named Laika, was launched by the former USSR on November 3, 1957.

Literacy Links

Letter Knowledge
○ Sing the song slowly so the children can hear the individual letters in the word *Bingo*.

Oral Language
○ Teach the children the American Sign Language sign for *dog* (page 121).

Print Awareness

○ Print *Bingo* on chart paper. Place your hand under each letter as it is mentioned in the song. Invite the children to make up other names for the farmer's dog. Print the other dog names on chart paper and name each letter as you write it.

Segmentation

○ Encourage the children to clap and count the letters in "Bingo." Ask the children to think of other five-letter names to substitute in the song.

Curriculum Connections

Blocks

○ Invite the children to build doghouses. Provide toy dogs to inhabit the houses.

○ Provide a ground cover, farm buildings, blocks, fences and plastic animals to create a farm. Be sure to add a dog, Bingo. Encourage the children to pretend they have a farm and a dog named Bingo.

Games

○ Play Farmer in the Dell (page 106).

Gross Motor

○ Provide dog bones and a dog dish. Place masking tape on the floor to create a throw line. Have the children toss the bones into the dish.

Language

○ Make and enlarge two or three photocopies of the dog from the Animal Patterns (page 113). Color them, cut them out, laminate them, and cut them into puzzle pieces. Place colored dots on the backs of puzzle pieces to help identify which pieces belong to which puzzle.

○ Photocopy the Animal Rhyming Word Cards (page 120) and the dog from the Animal Patterns (page 113). Color them, cut them out, and laminate them. Invite the children to find the cards that rhyme with *dog*.

Special Needs Adaptation: A child with special needs who is just learning language may find a rhyming activity too difficult. Adapt the activity by helping the child learn more about dogs. Review pet safety rules. Talk about different kinds of dogs. Bring in pictures of different dogs, and ask the child to make sentences about them. If the child is non-verbal or cognitively challenged, ask him to show you a small dog, a large dog, and so on. Help the child count the dog's legs or point to the dog's nose, mouth, and eyes.

Math

○ Provide dog collars and encourage the children to use them as measuring tools. How many things can the children find that are the same length as the collars?

Writing

○ Make Bingo Name Puzzles. Print *Bingo* on 4" x 10" strips of poster board. Leave a space between the letters. Laminate the strips and then make a puzzle by cutting between the letters on each strip. Suggest to the children that they put the puzzles together.

Home Connection

○ Send an index card home with the children and ask families to write the name of their dogs on the card. If they do not have a dog, have them write a name on the card that they think would be a good name for a dog. When the children return with the index cards, place them in the writing center for copying.

Bingo by Rosemary Wells
Good Dog, Carl by Alexandra Day
Harry the Dirty Dog by Gene Zion

Three White Mice
by Barbara Drolshagen and JoAnn Rajchel

(Tune: Three Blind Mice)
Three white mice,
Three white mice,
See how they dance,
See how they dance.
They danced and danced

For the farmer's wife,
Who played for them
On a silver fife.
Did you ever see
Such a sight in your life,
As three white mice,
Three white mice!
Three…white…mice!

Vocabulary

dance
farmer
fife
mice
three
sight
silver
white
wife

Theme Connections

Farms
Nursery Rhymes

Did You Know?

- ○ Mice are nocturnal animals and are more active at night than during the day. Rats and mice are rodents. Rats are extremely clean and intelligent pets.
- ○ Ancient Romans considered the rat good luck, and in China, the rat is considered a sign of prosperity.
- ○ Rats can swim.
- ○ Walt Disney created Mickey Mouse, based on inspiration from a little mouse he named Mortimer that lived in the garbage cans in the small studio where he worked. Mickey Mouse's original name was Mortimer but Walt's wife, Lillian, convinced him to change it. Walt chose the name Mickey because Mickey Rooney just happened to walk into Walt's office while Walt was contemplating a new name for Mortimer Mouse.

Literacy Links

Oral Language

- ○ Teach the children the American Sign Language sign for *mice* (page 122).

Oral Language/Print Awareness

○ Encourage children to name famous mice they know, for example, Mickey Mouse, Maisy, and Chuck E. Cheese. Make a list of the mice they name.

Phonological Awareness

○ Print the rhyming words *wife* and *fife* on chart paper. Point out that the words rhyme. Ask the children to think of other words that rhyme with *wife* and *fife* (*life* and *knife*).

Print Awareness

○ Print the song on chart paper. Move your hand beneath the words as you sing the song with the children.

Curriculum Connections

Art

○ Provide finger paint. Invite the children to use the paint to make fingerprints. Show them how to use markers to turn the fingerprints into mice.

Construction

○ Make a mouse puppet from a paper bag. Glue a brown construction paper triangle on the bottom of a small paper bag to make a mouse face. Add construction paper ears, eyes, nose, and whiskers. Invite children to use their puppets to re-enact the song.

Special Needs Adaptation: For children with motor challenges and/or fine motor skills problems, use a larger bag and larger pieces to make the mouse puppet. Some children can handle larger items more easily than smaller ones. Another alternative is to invite the child to ask a friend to help him make his mouse puppet. Working together on projects helps build social skills.

Fine Motor
O Provide white and pink playdough. Show the children how to shape mice from the white playdough. Provide small wiggle eyes, and use the pink playdough for the tail, nose, and insides of ears.

Games
O Play Old Gray Cat (page 106) with the children.

Language
O Photocopy the Animal Rhyming Word Cards (page 120) and the mouse from the Animal Patterns (page 114). Color them, cut them out, and laminate them. Encourage the children to find the words that rhyme with *mouse*.

 English Language Learner Strategy: Partner a proficient English speaker with an English language learner.

Math
O Make mice fingerprints on index cards. Make one mouse on the first card, two mice on the next card, three on the next card, and continue up to eight mice. Encourage the children to arrange the cards from the one with the least mice to the one with the most mice. Provide magnetic numerals from 1-8 and encourage the children to match the numerals to the cards.

 Special Needs Adaptation: If the child has only learned number concepts to three or four, give him the mice cards for the numbers 1-4. Placing the cards in order, from most to least, may be too abstract for some children. Instead, invite them to help you count the number of mice on each card.

Music and Movement
O Play Mousetrap as you would play London Bridge Is Falling Down. Two children are the "mousetrap," who clasp both hands and raise them over their heads for the other children to go under. The other children walk in a circle, one at a time going under the bridge, singing the following song to the tune of "The Ants Go Marching."

Cheese, cheese, cheese, cheese,
Cheese, cheese, cheese, cheese.
The mice go marching one by one, cheese please, cheese please.
The mice go marching one by one, cheese please, cheese please.
The mice go marching in search of cheese.
The little one stops, he has to sneeze
And he falls right in a trap that's full of cheese.

The trap closes, capturing whoever is under it on the last line of the song. The children who are the trap then gently move the trapped child back and forth while chanting:

Cheese, cheese, cheese, cheese,
Cheese, cheese, cheese, cheese.

The children who are the mousetrap release the trapped mouse when starting the verse again.

Snack
○ Encourage the children to follow the Mice Ice Cream Rebus Recipe (page 111) to make a yummy ice cream treat for snack.

Writing
○ Print *mice* on several index cards. Provide fingerpaint and encourage the children to cover the letters with fingerprints.

Home Connection

○ Suggest that the children ask their family members to think of words that rhyme with *wife* and *fife*.

Rags

with additional verses by Pam Schiller

(Tune: Five Little Ducks)
I have a dog and his name
   is Rags.
He eats so much that his
   tummy sags.
His ears flip-flop and his tail
   wig-wags,
And when he walks he zig,
   zig, zags!
Flip-flop,
Wig-wag,

My dog Rags he loves to play.
He rolls around in the mud
   all day.
I whistle for him but he
   won't obey!
He always runs the other way.
Flip-flop,
Wig-wag,
Zig, zag!
Hey, hey!

I have a horse and her name
   is Mop.
She runs so fast that it's hard
   to stop.
Her tail swish swashes and her
   feet clip-clop,
And when she runs she clippety,
   clops.
Swish, swash,
Clip, Clop,
Clippety-clop!

My horse Mop she loves to neigh.
She neighs and neighs in the
   fields all day.
I say, "Hey, you, come eat
   some hay!"
But all she says is, "Neigh,
   neigh, neigh."
Swish, swash,
Clip-clop,
Neigh, neigh!

Vocabulary

clip-clop
dog
flip-flops
horse
neigh
obey
sags
swash
swish
whistle
wig-wags

Theme Connections

Animals
Pets

Did You Know?

○ People all over the world love to pet dogs. In the United States and France, almost one in three families owns a dog.

○ There is a dog museum in St. Louis, Missouri, which was founded by the American Kennel Club. It has paintings, sculptures, and other works of art that are about dogs or have dogs in them. Many date back thousands of years!

○ Dogs always smell something, and dogs' sense of smell is about 1000 times better than a person's. Dogs can also hear a lot better than humans. They hear high-pitched sounds (like some insects make) that we cannot even detect. Dogs need a good sense of smell and hearing because their eyesight is not as good as a human's.

○ See pages 23 and 107 for more information about dogs.

Literacy Links

Letter Knowledge
❍ Print *clip* and *clop* and *plip* and *plop* on chart paper. *Which letter is different in each pair of words? Which letters are alike?*

Oral Language
❍ Discuss the many different ways that people call their dogs. Some people whistle, some call their dogs by name, and others simple say, "Here, dog." Encourage the children to try to whistle.
❍ Teach the children the American Sign Language signs for *dog* and *horse* (pages 121-122).

Phonological Awareness
❍ Print *wig* and *wag* and *zig* and *zag* on chart paper. Point out that each pair of words is a rhyming word pair. Help the children think of other words, including nonsense words, that rhyme with each pair of words.
❍ Discuss the *onomatopoeic* words in the song. (Onomatopoeic words imitate the sound they are describing.)

Curriculum Connections

Art
❍ Provide crayons and paper. Encourage the children to draw Rags or Mop.

Discovery
❍ Stitch 12" strips of elastic to each corner of each end of one yard of fabric to create a hammock. Place two chairs, back to back, three feet apart and then hook the elastic over the backs of the chairs. Provide blocks and other heavy objects for the children to put into the hammock to make it sag. *Can you make it sag to the floor? Do you think that Rags' tummy sags to the floor?*

Fine Motor
❍ Photocopy the dog from the Animal Patterns (page 113). Color it, cut it out, and glue it to the top of a small box with a lid (a stationery box works well). Use a matte knife (adult only) to cut a penny-size hole next to the dog's

Book Corner

My Pony by Susan
Jeffers
The Poky Little Puppy
by Janette
Sebring Lowrey
The Sleep Ponies by
Gudrun Ongman
That's My Dog by
Rick Walton

Games

○ Play Dog and Bone. Children sit in a circle. One child—IT—walks around the outside of the circle, carrying a paper or plastic bone. Eventually IT drops the bone behind a player. That player picks up the bone and chases IT around the circle. If she taps IT before they get around the circle, IT goes to the "doghouse" (center of the circle). If she doesn't, IT takes her place in the circle. The player with the bone becomes the new IT and the game continues.

Gross Motor

○ Use masking tape to make a zigzag line on the floor. Give the children a bone or a beanbag and challenge them to walk the zigzag line with the bone or beanbag on their head.

Language

○ Photocopy and enlarge text from magazines or newspaper clippings. Laminate the copies. Provide two different colors of dry-erase markers and have the children use one color to circle all the Rs (the first letter of Rags' name) and the other color to circle all the Ms (the first letter of Mop's name).

Listening

○ Provide noise-making items such as drumsticks, straws, blocks, castanets, and so on. Challenge the children to use the items to make "clip clop" sounds. *Which items work best?*

Sand and Water

○ Fill the sand and water table with dried grass or, if available, hay. Discuss the diet of horses.

Writing

○ Print *Rags* and *Mop* on chart paper. Provide magnetic letters and encourage the children to copy the names.

Home Connection

○ Encourage the children to talk with their families about pets their family members had when they were growing up.

Six White Ducks

Vocabulary

dive	six
ducks	sixth
fat	skinny
feather	splash
little	splish
quack	water
river	white
row	wibble
ruled	wobble

Theme Connections

Counting
Farms

Six white ducks that I once knew,
Fat ducks, skinny ducks, they were, too.
But the one little duck with the feather on her back,
She ruled the others with a quack, quack, quack!

Down to the river they would go,
Wibble, wobble, wibble, wobble, all in a row.
But the one little duck with the feather on her back,
She ruled the others with a quack, quack, quack!

Into the water they would dive,
Splish, splash, splish, splash, one through five.
But the sixth little duck with the feather on her back,
She ruled the others with a quack, quack, quack!

Did You Know?

- There are over 52 species of ducks common to North America, including the common mallard and rarer species, like the white-headed duck.
- Ducks form large flocks during the winter and pair off during the breeding season. Males and females build nests lined with down.
- Ducklings leave the nest quickly, and in the spring they are frequently seen following their mothers, all in a row.
- White ducks commonly kept as pets are Peking ducks. They were first brought from China to the United States in 1873 to raise for meat. Mallards, with their green heads and beautiful markings, are the most common and widely found wild ducks.
- See pages 91 and 107 for additional information about ducks.

Literacy Links

Comprehension

❍ Make a KWL Chart for ducks. To make the chart, draw three columns on a sheet of chart paper. At the top of the first column print "What We Know." At the top of the second column print "What We Want to Know." At the top of the third column print "What We Learned." Fill in the first two columns before studying ducks and fill in the last column after studying ducks.

Oral Language

❍ Provide a feather for each child. Ask the children to put their feathers *on* their heads, *under* their feet, *on top* of their hands, *under* their arms, *behind* their backs, and so on.

> ✓ **Special Needs Adaptation:** If the child does not understand the positional words, model the motions for her. Repeat out loud what you are doing, "The feather is *under* my foot," "The feather is *on top* of my head." For children with oral language skill challenges, place the feather in a container, such as plastic bowl. Say, "The feather is *in* the bowl." Take the feather out of the bowl and say, "The feather is *out of* the bowl." Ask the child to put the feather *in* the bowl or take it *out of* the bowl. Reinforce the concepts of *in* and *out* by putting other items in the bowl and taking them out.

❍ Teach the children the American Sign Language sign for *duck* (page 121)

Phonological Awareness

❍ Discuss *quack*. Explain that *quack* is an *onomatopoeic* word, a word that imitates the sound it is describing. Ask children to think of other animal sounds that are onomatopoeic words.

❍ Print *wibble* and *wobble* on chart paper. Ask the children to identify the letters in each word. *Which letter is different in each word? What happens to the word if you insert the letter "a" in place of the "i" or the "o"? Insert a "u" in place of the "i" or the "o"?*

Curriculum Connections

Art

❍ Provide tempera paint, paper, and large feathers and encourage the children to paint with the feathers.

Discovery

○ Provide feathers and a basket. Have the children try to drop the feathers from above their heads and get them to land inside the basket. If the feathers go astray, suggest blowing gently to guide them into the basket. *Is it easier if you drop the feather from your waist?*

Games

○ Place a strip of masking tape on one end of a table and another strip at the other end of the table, creating a start and finish line. Place two feathers at one end of the table, one on each side of the start line. Invite two children to use a turkey baster to blow the feathers to the opposite end of the table.

Gross Motor

○ Invite the children to crawl along a line of masking tape with a feather on their back.

Math

○ Print the numerals 1-6 on plastic eggs. Provide a bowl of buttons. Have the children place the number of buttons into each egg as indicated by the numeral on the outside of the egg.

Science

○ Fill plastic eggs with objects of different weights. Encourage the children to arrange the eggs according to weight, lightest to heaviest. Try rolling the eggs. *Which eggs are easiest to roll?*

Writing

○ Provide a sturdy feather that can be used for a quill and small bowls of tempera paint. Make a diagonal cut on the stiff end of the feather. Show the children how to use the feather as a quill. Print *duck* on index cards and invite the children to use their quills to trace over the letters.

Home Connection

○ Suggest that families take their children to a local pond to feed the ducks.

Little Quack by
Lauren
Thompson
One Smart Goose by
Caroline Jane
Church

SONGS AND ACTIVITIES

I Met a Bear

(Tune: Sippin' Cider Through
   a Straw)
*(The children echo the words in
   parentheses.)*
The other day (The other day)
I met a bear, (I met a bear)
A great big bear (A great big bear)
A way out there. (A way
   out there)

All sing:
The other day, I met a bear,
A great big bear, a way out there.

He looked at me. (He looked
   at me)
I looked at him. (I looked at him)
He sized me up. (He sized
   me up)
I sized him up. (I sized him up)

All sing:
He looked at me. I looked at
   him.
He sized me up. I sized him up.

He said to me, (He said to me)
"Why don't you run? ("Why
   don't you run?)
I think it's time (I think it's time)
To have some fun." (To have
   some fun.")

All sing:
He said to me "Why don't
   you run?
I think it's time to have some
   fun. *(all sing)*

I said to him, (I said to him)
"That's a good idea." ("That's a
   good idea.")
"Now legs get going, ("Now legs
   get going,)
Get me out of here." (Get me out
   of here.")

All sing:
I said to him, "That's a
   good idea."
"Now legs get going, get me out
   of here."

And so I ran (And so I ran)
Away from there, (Away from
   there)
But right behind me (But right
   behind me)
Was that bear. (Was that bear)

All sing:
And so I ran away from there,
But right behind me was
   that bear.

In front of me (In front of me)
There was a tree, (There was
   a tree)
A great big tree (A great big tree)
Oh glory be! (Oh glory be!)

All sing:
In front of me there was a tree,
A great big tree, oh glory be!

The lowest branch (The lowest
   branch)
Was ten feet up, (Was ten
   feet up)

Vocabulary

bear
branch
end
fret
frown
jump
lowest
luck
miss
sized me up
trust

Theme Connections

Humor
Make-Believe

So I thought I'd jump (So I
thought I'd jump)
And trust my luck. (And trust
my luck.)

All sing:
The lowest branch was ten
feet up,
So I thought I'd jump and trust
my luck.

And so I jumped (And so
I jumped)
Into the air, (Into the air)
But I missed that branch (But I
missed that branch)
Away up there. (Away up there.)

All sing:
And so I jumped into the air,
But I missed that branch, away
up there.

Now don't you fret (Now don't
you fret)

And don't you frown, (And don't
you frown)
I caught that branch (I caught
that branch)
On the way back down! (On the
way back down)

All sing:
Now don't you fret and don't you
frown,
I caught that branch on the way
back down!

This is the end. (This is the end)
There is no more. (There is no
more)
Unless I see (Unless I see)
That bear once more. (That bear
once more)

All sing:
This is the end. There ain't
no more,
Unless I see that bear once more.
(That great big bear!)

Did You Know?

○ There are many different species of bears, including the brown bear, grizzly bear, black bear, and polar bear. Bears live in all parts of the world except for Antarctica, Africa, and Australia.

○ Bears are large animals. They have very strong legs, big heads, and small eyes. They have good close-up vision.

○ Female bears are called sows and male bears are called boars. A group of bears is referred to as a sloth of bears. Baby bears are called cubs. When cubs are born, they are about the size of a squirrel.

○ Most bears eat nuts, fruits, berries, plants, insects, honey, fish, and other animals. They eat a lot of food to prepare for winter.

○ Bears make or find dens in the winter when they hibernate.

○ Bears can run uphill and downhill and on flat ground. Lean bears can run faster than 30 miles per hour. Fat bears in their winter coats overheat and tire quickly when running.

Literacy Links

Comprehension

❍ Ask the children to generate a list of questions they have about bears; for example, "How large can bears grow?" "What do they eat?" or "Where do they live?" Provide a good reference book about bears. Help the children find answers to their questions using the book. If answers aren't found in the book try another book or use the internet.

 Special Needs Adaptation: Adapt this activity for children with special needs by showing them a picture of a bear. Instead of asking him to generate a list of questions, provide a few facts about bears, such as what bears eat.

Oral Language

❍ Talk about bears, their size, their weight, and so on. Have the children demonstrate walking like a bear. Explain that bears have more balance when they walk on all four feet.

❍ Teach the children the American Sign Language sign for *bear*.

Phonological Awareness

❍ Challenge the children to think of words that rhyme with bear. Nonsense words are acceptable.

bear

Curriculum Connections

Dramatic Play

❍ Make a bear cave by draping a dark sheet or blanket over a table. Provide stuffed bears to live inside.

Gross Motor

❍ Hang a small branch from the ceiling 10' from the ground. Encourage the children to jump to reach the branch. Does anyone get close? Why not?

Health and Safety

O   Teach the children bear safety.

Language

O   Photocopy the bear from the Animal Pattern Cards (page 119) and the Rhyming Word Cards (page 120). Challenge the children to find the cards that rhyme with *bear*.

Math

O   Cut a 10' piece of yarn to represent the height that the person in the song jumped to catch a branch. Lay the yarn on the floor. Have the children see how many of them can stand on the yarn. Ask them to lie down head to feet beside the yarn. How many children does it take to make a line longer than the yarn?

Music and Movement

O   Play classical music and have the children dance like bears. *Are bears graceful dancers or clumsy dancers?* Let the children decide.

   Special Needs Adaptation: If a child has physical limitations, give him a scarf and ask him to wave his scarf to the music instead of dancing.

Snack

O   Invite the children to follow the Bear Claw Rebus Recipe (page 109) to make their snack.

Writing

O   Print *bear* on index cards. Provide small leaves and twigs for the children to use to cover the letters.

Home Connections

O   Encourage the children to tell their families about bear safety.
O   Ask families to send a stuffed bear to school with their children. Have the children arrange the bears by size, sort them by color, and weigh them to find the heaviest. Make sure to have a few extra bears for children who do not have one or forget to bring one in.

From Head to Toe by Eric Carle
I Met a Bear by Dan Yaccarino
The Other Day I Met a Bear by Russell Ayto

Ten Little Monkeys

One, two, three little monkeys,
Four, five, six little monkeys,
Seven, eight, nine little
    monkeys,
Ten little monkeys at the zoo.

One little monkey doing
    some tricks.
Two little monkeys
    picking up sticks.
Three little monkeys
    standing in lines.
Four little monkeys
    swinging on vines.

One, two, three little monkeys,
Four, five, six little monkeys,
Seven, eight, nine little
    monkeys,
Ten little monkeys at the zoo.

Vocabulary

eight
five
four
monkey
nine
one
seven
six
stick
swinging
ten
three
trick
two
vines
zoo

Theme Connections

Counting
Zoos

Did You Know?

- The monkeys of the world are divided into two groups: the monkeys of Africa and Asia and the monkeys of Central and South America. The first group has long thick tails that help them balance while they swing through the forest. The second group of monkeys, like the familiar spider monkey, have tails that can grasp and are used like hands and feet to help them swing through the treetops and dangle upside down.
- Monkeys are *primates*, a category of mammals. They are warm-blooded and have fur. Primates are social animals. They enjoy spending time with their friends and family.
- A group of monkeys is called a *troop*.
- All monkeys like to be clean. Troops of monkeys have a "barber" monkey to clean their fur. The barber monkey's reward is the bugs in his customer's hair.
- Monkeys peel their bananas because they don't eat the skin.

Literacy Links

Comprehension
○ Discuss monkeys. Print *monkey* in the middle of a sheet of chart paper. Draw a circle around it. Ask the children to tell you what they know about monkeys and print their information on lines that extend from the circle.

Listening
○ Sing the song again and tell the children to stand and sit every time they hear the word *monkey* in the song.
○ Read the action story, "Monkey See, Monkey Do" (page 104). Encourage the children to follow the directions in the story to act it out.

Oral Language
○ Teach the children the American Sign Language sign for *monkey* (page 122).

Phonological Awareness
○ Help the children identify the rhyming word pairs in the song; for example, *tricks* and *sticks*, and *lines* and *vines*. Challenge them to add more rhyming words to each rhyming pair.

Print Awareness
○ Print the song on chart paper using numerals instead of number words. Move your hand under the words as you sing. Point out that the print moves from left to right and top to bottom. Call attention to the numerals and discuss the difference between numerals and letters.

Curriculum Connections

Dramatic Play
○ Provide zoo props, stuffed animals, aprons, feeding buckets, and a zookeeper's hat, for the children to use for pretend play. Encourage the children to take care of the zoo animals, especially the monkeys.

Field Trip
○ Take a trip to the zoo. Count the monkeys. Discuss safe behavior at the zoo. If you can't take a real trip to the zoo, take a pretend trip.

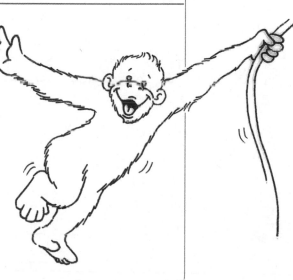

Fine Motor

❍ Provide a basket of small sticks. Encourage the children to take off their shoes and pick up the sticks with their toes. Remind the children about the monkey's ability to use its toes like fingers.

Games

❍ Invite the children to play Monkey Nonsense. Appoint one child to be the guesser and have the guesser leave the room. Select one child to be the lead monkey. The rest of the children are also monkeys. When the guesser returns to the room the lead monkey begins to do monkey antics and all the other monkeys copy the antics. If she scratches her head, the rest of the children have to scratch their heads. The guesser tries to figure out who is the lead monkey. The monkey should try not to get caught changing the action. If the monkey gets caught, then she becomes the next guesser.

❍ Teach the children how to play Monkey See, Monkey Do. Have each child select a partner. Ask partners to face each other. One child acts like a monkey and the second child copies the monkey antics.

> **Special Needs Adaptation:** Playing cooperatively with a friend can be difficult for a child with disabilities. Practice playing Monkey See, Monkey Do with the child before he plays with a partner. Model each step of the game. If the child seems unsure of what to do, take his hands and help him imitate what you are doing. When selecting a peer buddy to play with the child, identify a child who will be patient and kind to the child with disabilities. Talk to the peer buddy ahead of time. Suggest things the peer buddy may ask the child to imitate in the game.

Math

❍ Present math problem-solving stories to the children. Here are some examples.
  ○ There were four monkeys in the monkey cage. The zookeeper put two more monkeys in the cage. How many monkeys are in the cage now?
  ○ There are two monkeys swinging on a vine. Three monkeys climb on the same vine. How many monkeys are on the vine?
  ○ Three monkeys were eating bananas. Three more monkeys joined the feast. How many monkeys are eating bananas?

Monkey See, Monkey Do by Marc Gave
Monkey See, Monkey Do by Dana Regan
Ten Little Monkeys: A Counting Storybook by Keith Faulkner

Movement

○ Invite the children to act out "Five Little Monkeys Sitting In a Tree" (page 112). Help the children think of an alternate ending where the monkeys escape.

Snack

○ Invite the children to use the Monkey Treat Rebus Recipe (page 112) to make their snack.

Writing

○ Print *monkey* and *zoo* on chart paper and encourage the children to use magnetic letters to copy the words.

Home Connection

○ Suggest the children teach their families how to play Monkey See, Monkey Do.

Three Tricky Turtles

by Pam Schiller

(Tune: Three Blind Mice)
Three pokey turtles.
Three pokey turtles.
See how they move.
See how they move.
They all decided
To race a deer.
Their friends and family began to cheer.
The deer got beat by a trick I hear.
Three tricky turtles.
Three tricky turtles.

Vocabulary

cheer	three
decided	trick
deer	tricky
pokey	turtle
race	

Theme Connections

Counting
Folk Tales

Did You Know?

○ About 270 species of turtles, tortoises, and terrapins live worldwide in tropical and temperate zones.

○ All turtles and tortoises have a shell that is part of their skeletons. The shell prevents moisture loss and absorbs heat to warm these cold-blooded animals.

○ Turtles and tortoises have adapted in different ways to adjust to their environments. Terrestrial turtles have short legs that are adapted for walking. Sea turtles have flipper-like feet that help them swim.

○ Terrestrial turtles, like the box turtle, have large shells that provide room to pull limbs and head inside for protection. Sea turtles and pond turtles have streamlined shells for swimming. These shells don't provide room for the turtle to pull its limbs inside.

○ Turtles have a plodding steady gait that sooner or later gets them to where they are going.

Literacy Links

Listening/Comprehension

○ Read the listening story, "Tortoise Wins a Race" (page 105). This song is about the race in the story. Ask questions at the end of the story. *How would the story be different if the deer had figured out the trick? What was the trick? Would a deer ever race a turtle?*

Oral Language

○ Talk about turtles. Ask children to tell you what they know about turtles.

Phonological Awareness

○ Help the children think of other adjectives to describe *turtles,* such as *slow, happy, green,* and so on. Challenge them to think of an alliterative adjective (in this case, one that starts with "t"), for example, *tame, tiny, topsy-turvey,* and so on.

 Special Needs Adaptation: If the child with special needs has limited language ability, suggest that she make a sentence about a turtle. You may have to demonstrate. Ask the child to repeat the sentence after you. Next, add more words to the sentence. Be sure to include a few adjectives. After the child is more comfortable with the words, see if she can give you an attribute, such as a color, size, or another descriptive word. Use that word in a sentence.

Phonological Awareness/Letter Knowledge

○ Print *Three Tricky Turtles* on chart paper. Ask the children to identify the first letter in each word. Point out that when several words in a phrase of sentence all begin with the same letter sound it is called *alliteration.* Have the children say "Three Tricky Turtles" three times quickly.

Curriculum Connections

Art

○ Give the children oval sponges, paper, and finger paint. Have them dip the sponge into the paint and then press it onto their paper to create a turtle shell. Have them make a thumbprint head, legs, and tail to create a turtle.

Construction

○ Invite the children to make turtles. Give each child a small paper bowl. Provide green tempera paint and brown construction paper. Have the children paint their bowls to create a turtle shell and then cut out a head, legs, and a tail from the construction paper and glue them onto the bowl.

Top view →

Book Corner

Fine Motor

○ Provide a bowl of half walnut shells to represent turtle shells. Show the children how to spin the shells.

Games

○ Provide three half walnut shells, representing turtle shells, and a button. Put a button under one of the walnut shells and shuffle the shells around. Ask children to guess which shell the button is under.

Gross Motor

○ Draw a turtle shell on a piece of cardboard or poster board. Cut a hole in the middle of the shell and invite the children to stand behind a throw line and toss a beanbag through the hole.

Language

○ Give the children plastic turtles and a deer. Invite them to re-enact the story "Tortoise Wins a Race" (page 105).

Snack

○ Give the children round crackers, peanut butter, raisins, and pretzels. Show them how to create an edible turtle by putting two crackers together with the peanut butter and then add a raisin for the head and pretzels for legs. **Allergy Warning:** Check for peanut allergies.

Writing

○ Print *turtle* and *deer* on index cards. Provide a tray of sand and craft sticks. Encourage the children to use the stick as a writing tool and copy the words in the sand.

Home Connection

○ Encourage the children to tell their families the story, "Tortoise Wins a Race."

Sweetly Sings the Donkey

Vocabulary

break of day
donkey
hee-haw
sing
sweetly

Theme Connections

Farms
Sounds

(Tune: Down by the Station)
Sweetly sings the donkey
At the break of day.
If you do not feed him,
This is what he'll say:
"Hee-haw, hee-haw,
Hee-haw, hee-haw, hee-haw,
Hee-haw, hee-haw,
Hee-haw, hee-haw, hee-haw!"

Did You Know?

○ Donkeys are related to horses, ponies, and zebras.
○ Donkeys are unfairly thought to be stubborn and stupid, but people who keep them say that they are highly intelligent and single-minded, meaning that, unlike horses, they cannot be commanded into dangerous situations.
○ Female donkeys are called jennies, males are jacks, and babies are foals (jack foal or jenny foal).
○ They have a loud, distinctive braying voice that sounds like "hee-haw." In the wild, donkeys live far apart from each other. This may be why they have developed amazing voices that can carry up to a mile and a half or three kilometers. Their large ears help them hear sounds from a long distance.
○ In some countries, a donkey is a person's most prized possession. The donkey is the owner's tractor, family car, shopping cart, guard dog, and companion.

Literacy Links

Oral Language

○ Discuss the phrase "at the break of day." *What does it mean? Why did the donkey sing at the break of day? What other animal sings at the break of day?* (Rooster)

donkey

○ Talk about donkeys. Create a KWL chart as follows. Draw three columns on chart paper. Label the first column "What We Know." Label the second column "What We Want to Know." Label the third column "What We Learned." Fill in the first two columns with what the children already know and want to know about donkeys. Fill in the last column at the end of your study of donkeys.

○ Teach the children the American Sign Language sign for *donkey*.

Print Awareness

○ Print the song on chart paper. Move your hands under the words as you sing the song. Point out the top-to-bottom and left-to-right progression of the print.

Curriculum Connections

Blocks

○ Invite the children to build a farm. Have them discuss all the ways a donkey might help on their farm.

Construction

○ Encourage the children to cut large donkey ears from construction paper and then glue them onto a headband. Suggest that the children take their ears outdoors and wear them while trying out some donkey kicks (see Outdoors).

Games

○ Play Pin the Tail on the Donkey. If children do not want to be blindfolded, then allow them to close their eyes instead.

Listening

○ Provide a tape recorder. Encourage children to sing and record donkey songs. Can they sing "Sweetly Sings the Donkey" using only *hee-haws*?

Math

○ Give the children playdough and the letter U from a set of magnetic letters. Show them how to roll their dough into a flat surface and then use the U, representing a donkey's footprint, to create a pattern. For example, they may make two U shapes going up and then one facing down and repeat.

Book Corner

*The Donkey's
Christmas Song*
by Nancy Tafuri
*Sylvester and the
Magic Pebble* by
William Steig

Music

O Sing morning songs with the children, such as "Good Morning to You" or "Lazy Mary, Will You Get Up." Also sing nighttime songs, such as "Rockabye, Baby" and "Hush, Little Baby."

Outdoors

O Show the children how to place their hands on the ground and then kick up their heels like a donkey.

Sand and Water

O Fill the table with "donkey food" (hay). Encourage the children to hide small items in the hay and then have their friends find them.

 Special Needs Adaptation: For the child who may have difficulty finding hidden objects, be sure part of an object shows through the hay, or hide larger objects. If the child seems hesitant to touch the hay, play the game with him and reach into the hay. Remember to verbalize what you find. For example, "Look _____ (use the child's name), I found a truck."

Writing

O Print *donkey* on index cards. Provide tempera paint and pipe cleaners with one end shaped into a horseshoe shape (or U). Have the children dip the pipe cleaners into the paint and then stamp them over the letters so that the word *donkey* is covered in donkey footprints.

donkey

← Paint

Home Connection

O Encourage the children to talk with their families about why donkeys sing at the break of day. They may also want to tell their families what the donkey sings (*hee haw*).

Three Bears' Rap

Out in the forest in a wee little
cottage lived the three bears.
One was the Mama Bear, one
was the Papa Bear,
And one was the wee bear.

Out of the forest came a walking,
stalking, pretty little Goldilocks
And upon the door she was
a-knockin'.
Knock, knock, knock.
But no one was there, unh-unh,
no one was there.
So she walked right in, had
herself a bowl.
She didn't care, unh-unh, she
didn't care.

Home, home, home came the
three bears.

"Someone's been eating my
porridge," said the
Mama Bear.
"Someone's been eating my
porridge," said the Papa Bear.
"Baa-baa, barebear," said the
little wee bear.
"Someone's broken my
chair!" Crash!

Just then Goldilocks she woke up.
She broke up the party and she
beat it out of there.
"Goodbye, goodbye, goodbye,"
said the Mama Bear.
"Goodbye, goodbye, goodbye,"
said the Papa Bear.
"Baa-baa, Barebear," said the
little wee bear.
That's the story of the three little
bears—yeah!

Vocabulary

bears
beat
chair
cottage
forest
home
mama
papa
porridge
stalking
story
wee

Theme Connections

Families
Traditional Tales

Did You Know?

○ The story of the Three Bears and an intruder has been around for at least two centuries.
○ The first recorded version of "the Three Bears" was published by Robert Southey in 1837 in a collection of essays titled, *The Doctor*. The fourth volume contained "Story of the Three Bears." This version was so influential that for a time it was thought to be the origin of the story before proof of the earlier versions was discovered by scholars. Southey's version featured an old woman as the intruder, so this story was not quite yet like the version best known today (Opie 1974, 199-200).

Opie, Iona and Peter. 1974. *The classic fairy tales*. New York: Oxford University Press.

Literacy Links

Comprehension

○ Ask questions about the events in the song. *Whose chair got broken? Why did Goldilocks run away? Have you ever been frightened like Goldilocks was? How would the song be different if Goldilocks had already known the three bears?*

○ Encourage the children to sequence the events in the song. Read the story of "The Three Bears." Do the events happen in the same sequence?

 English Language Learner Strategy: Pantomime each activity in the story of "The Three Bears." Provide props and then have the English language learners pantomime as you read the story.

Oral Language

○ Show the children a picture of Goldilocks. Ask them where they think Goldilocks got her name. *Why is she called Goldilocks?* Print *Goldilocks* on chart paper. Separate the words *gold* and *locks*. Explain to the children that locks can refer to hair.

○ Teach the children the American Sign Language sign for *bear* (page 121).

Phonological Awareness

○ Discuss the sound of Goldilocks knocking on the door (*cluck, cluck, cluck*). Explain that sounds that imitate the sound they are describing are called *onomatopoeic* sounds. *What other sounds could have been used to sound like a knock on the door?* (*bam, tap, rap*)

Curriculum Connections

Blocks

○ Encourage the children to build the three bear's cottage.

Construction

○ Invite the children to make Goldilocks Puppets. Give each child a six-inch paper plate and a craft stick. Provide construction paper, markers, wiggle eyes, and gold-colored yarn. Encourage the children to create facial features on their plate from the provided materials and then glue the yarn onto the plate to create Goldilocks' hair. Have them glue their plates to the craft sticks to finish their puppets.

Book Corner

Goldilocks and the Three Bears by Jan Brett
Goldilocks and the Three Bears by Valeri Gorbachev
Goldilocks and the Three Bears by James Marshall
The Three Bears by Paul Galdone

Discovery

○ Provide a wooden surface (tabletop or large block) and several items, such as drumsticks, small blocks, straws, and washers to use for knocking. Encourage the children to knock on the wooden surface with each item. *Which item makes the loudest sound? Which item makes the softest sound? Which item would you use if you were trying to knock softly so that you wouldn't wake up a baby? Which item would you use if there was someone in the house playing loud music?*

Dramatic Play

○ Provide sleeping bags and other bedding and invite the children to make three beds, one for each bear.

Language

○ Photocopy the bear picture in the Animal Patterns (page 119). Enlarge two of the patterns to make three different size bears. Color them, mount each bear on a different color of construction paper, cut them out, and laminate them. Cut each bear into puzzle pieces. Invite the children to work the puzzles. Talk with the children as they work the puzzles. Discuss the way the puzzle pieces fit together.

Math

○ Provide a basket of items, such as buttons, tiles, washers, crayons, and so on. Ask the children to use these items to make sets of three items. Show the children how their sets of three can be configured into two crayons and one crayon, or three crayons and no crayons and still remain three crayons.

Snack

○ Serve Cream of Wheat or oatmeal for snack. Talk about *porridge*. Remind children that porridge is a hot, thick cereal. It can also be a hot, well-cooked vegetable soup.

Home Connection

○ Suggest that the children ask their family members to tell them the story of "The Three Bears" for a bedtime story. If family members do not know the story, suggest that the child tell the story to his or her family.

Gray Squirrel

additional verse by Richele Bartkowiak

Vocabulary

acorn
balance
bushy
funny
gray
higher
nose
squirrel
swish
tail
telephone wire
toes
wrinkle

Theme Connections

Colors
Seasons

(Stand to sing this song.)
Gray squirrel, gray squirrel,
Swish your bushy tail. *(place hand behind back and swish it like a tail)*
Gray squirrel, gray squirrel,
Swish your bushy tail.
Wrinkle up your funny nose, *(wrinkle nose)*
Hold an acorn in your toes. *(pinch thumb and fingers together)*
Gray squirrel, gray squirrel,
Swish your bushy tail. *(place hand behind back
   and swish it like a tail)*

Gray squirrel, gray squirrel,
Swish your bushy tail. *(place hand behind
   back and swish it like a tail)*
Gray squirrel, gray squirrel,
Swish your bushy tail.
Balance on that telephone wire.
   (point up)
Don't look down when you get higher.
   (close eyes)
Gray squirrel, gray squirrel,
Swish your bushy tail. *(place hand behind back and swish it like a tail)*

Did You Know?

- There are some 300 varieties of squirrels around the world. In North America, there are ten, including red/brown squirrels that live in evergreen trees and gray squirrels that lives in woods of oaks, ashes, and beeches.
- Squirrels vary in size. For example, the gray squirrel can be up to three times as large as the red squirrel, but smaller than a fox squirrel. A newborn gray squirrel is about one inch long and weighs about an ounce. The size of an adult gray squirrel is about 18 inches, weighing up to a pound or more.
- Squirrels typically live in trees. The homes in the treetops are called *dreys* and sometimes consist of two rooms and a nursery!
- The gray squirrel's main diet consists of nuts, seeds, and fruit.
- Squirrels chew on tree branches to sharpen and clean their teeth.
- Squirrels communicate through a series of chirps. The frequency, and the duration of the notes communicate everything from laughter to alarm.

Literacy Links

Letter Knowledge
❍ Print *squirrel* on chart paper. Ask the children to identify the letters. *Which letter shows up twice?*

Oral Language
❍ Define words in the song that may be new vocabulary to the children. For example, *swish, bushy, wrinkle, acorn* and so on. Encourage the children to talk about what they know about squirrels.
❍ Show the children an acorn. Discuss its origin. Crack it open and show them the yellow meat inside. Explain that it is not suitable for eating but that it can be used as an ink or to create a dye.
❍ Talk about squirrels. *Where do they live? What do they eat? What sounds do they make?*
❍ Teach the children the American Sign Language sign for *squirrel* (page 123).

Phonological Awareness
❍ Ask the children to think of words that rhyme with *squirrel*.

Curriculum Connections

Note: If acorns are not available, use marbles for any of the activities.

Art
❍ Provide tempera paint, paper, a shallow box, and acorns. Invite the children to make designs with acorns. Place a sheet of paper in the bottom of a shallow box. Place acorns in a cup of tempera paint. Use a plastic spoon to put an acorn in the box. Have the children tilt the box back and forth to roll the acorn so that it makes a design on their paper.

Construction
❍ Provide 1" x 12" strips of brown butcher paper or paper from brown paper bags. Have the children gather the strips to create a bushy tail. When children have enough strips to make a bushy tail, wrap masking tape around one end of their strips to keep the strips together. Have the children swish their "tails."

Earl the Squirrel by
Don Freeman
*Gray Squirrel's
Daring Day* by
Geri Harrington
A Squirrel's Tale by
Richard Fowler

Dramatic Play
○ Provide a mirror. Encourage the children to stand in front of the mirror and do squirrel antics like wrinkling their nose, tiptoeing across telephone wires, swishing their bushy tail, and holding an acorn in their toes.

Fine Motor
○ Provide a box of acorns. Have the children take off their shoes and pick up acorns with their toes. *Is it easy or difficult? Why?*

Gross Motor
○ Provide a balance beam. Have the children pretend it is a telephone wire and walk across it as a squirrel might. If a balance beam is not available, place a strip of masking tape on the floor and encourage the children to walk along it on their toes.

Math
○ Provide acorns and 10 plastic cups with the numerals 1–10 written on them. Have the children count the designated number of acorns into each cup.

Science
○ Provide a variety of nuts and a muffin tin and ask the children to sort the nuts.

Writing
○ Print *squirrel* on sheets of paper. Provide yellow chalk (representing the meat inside an acorn) for the children to trace over the letters.

Home Connection

○ Encourage the children to look for squirrels around their homes. Ask families to take their children to a local park to see squirrels. When children return to school discuss how many squirrels each child saw. If someone didn't see any squirrels, talk about the habitat of the squirrel. Maybe squirrels don't live in everyone's neighborhood.

Animal Fair

I went to the animal fair.
The birds and the beasts were there.
The big baboon by the light of the moon
Was combing his auburn hair.
You should have seen the monk.
He sat on the elephant's trunk.
The elephant sneezed and fell to her knees.
And what became of the monk, the monk?
Oh, what became of the monk?

Vocabulary

animal
auburn
baboon
beast
birds
elephant
fair
knees
light
monk
moon
sneezed
trunk

Theme Connections

Celebrations
Humor

Did You Know?

○ A fair is an exhibition, usually competitive, of farm products and livestock. In the United States, fairs are often combined with entertainment and held annually by a counties and states.

○ A fair can also be a periodic gathering of buyers and sellers in an appointed place.

○ A fair may be an exhibition to raise money, often for a charitable purpose, by the sale of merchandise.

○ The first world's fair was held in London in 1851, with the goal of allowing people to explore the world outside of their everyday lives—to experience unfamiliar cultures, new scientific advancements, and new inventions. As times change, the world's fairs have changed too. They continue to reflect both the commercial needs of their times while also presenting the evolving ideals, hopes, and aspirations of people.

Literacy Links

Oral Language

○ Discuss fairs. Show photos, if possible. *Who has ever been to a fair? What do you see at a fair? What can you eat at a fair?*

○ Provide photos of baboons, elephants, and monkeys. Talk about each animal. *How do they move? What do they eat? What sounds do they make?*

○ Teach the children the American Sign Language signs for *monkey* and *elephant*.

elephant

Phonological Awareness

○ Encourage the children to help identify rhyming words in the song; for example, *fair/there/hair, moon/raccoon,* and *monk/trunk*.

○ Print *birds* and *beasts* on chart paper. Underline the letter "b" in birds and beast. Point out that the repetition of the beginning letter sounds is called *alliteration*. Print a list of animals that begin with the letter "b", such as *bee, bear, baboon, bat, badger, beetle, boar,* and *bison*. Distinctly pronounce the beginning sound /b/ of each animal.

> ✔ **Special Needs Adaptation:** Help the children become more familiar with the letter "b." Invite the children to go with you on a discovery walk around the classroom. Select three or four items that begin with the letter "b", such as a book, block, and ball. Talk about how each word starts with the letter "b". Build vocabulary by asking the child questions about each item. Instead of printing a list of animals that begin with "b", bring in pictures of two or three animals that begin with "b". Invite the children to say each animal's name. Practice these activities several times during the week.

Print Awareness

○ Print the song on chart paper. Move your hand under the words as you sing the song. Point out the left-to-right and top-to-bottom progression of the words.

Curriculum Connections

Blocks

○ Invite the children to build a fairground. Encourage them to make a place for animals, concession stands, and rides.

Dramatic Play

○ Provide fishing poles, a large box, and several small prizes. Make a fishing pole by tying yarn to one end of a cardboard tube from a coat hanger. Tie a small bucket or paper cup to the other end. Make a wall (barrier) with a large cardboard box. Cut out the bottom, top, and one side of the box. Use the three remaining side to make a barrier by standing the box

upright. Make sure the box is not taller than the children. Encourage the children to pretend they are playing a fishing game at a fair. Have one child hide behind the barrier and put prizes in the bucket while the other children "fish."

Fine Motor

❍ Provide strips of auburn (reddish brown) yarn, a craft stick, and a small paper plate. Encourage the children to draw a baboon face on the plates. Have the children glue the auburn yarn (hair) around the face. Glue the baboon head onto a craft stick to create a baboon puppet.

Math

❍ Cut out colorful balloons from construction paper. Add yarn strings to each balloon. Have the children create bouquets of balloons in sets of three, four, five, six, seven, and eight.

❍ Make pretend candied apples. Cut red apples from construction paper. Glue the apples to craft sticks. Make caramel coating (covers) for the apples by cutting half-circles, slightly wider than the apples, from brown construction paper. Glue two half-circles together to form a pocket that will slip over the top of the apple and cover it half way like caramel sauce. Print numerals on the caramel covers and dots on the craft sticks. Have the children place the caramel numeral cover on the apple to match the dots on the stick.

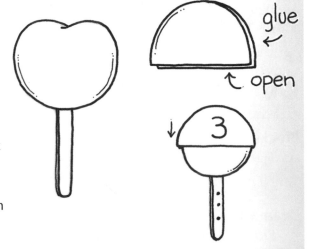

 English Language Learner Strategy: Ask a child who is proficient in English to work cooperatively with an English language learner to complete the activity together.

Music and Movement

○ Teach the children the Calliope Song. Divide children into four groups. Instruct group one to make an "um pa pa, um pa pa" sound while they bend their knees to move up and down. Have group two make an "um tweedli-dee, um tweedli-dee" sound while moving up and down on their tiptoes. Ask group three to make an "um shhh, um shhh" sound while swaying from side to side. Have group four hum the music while turning slowly in a circle.

○ Provide a light source to represent the moon. Have the children dance between the light source and the moon to create moon shadows. Play carnival music while they dance.

Sand and Water/Games

○ Create a Fair Duck Pond by placing rubber ducks in the water table. Place colored dots on the bottoms of the ducks. Make two of each color. Encourage the children to play a matching game by trying to catch two ducks that have the same color dot on the bottom.

Snack

○ Invite the children to make homemade ice cream. Have the children follow the Animal Ice Cream Rebus (page 108) to make an ice cream snack.

Home Connection

○ Encourage the children to talk with their families about fairs they have visited.

Animal Fair by
 Anthony Browne
The Animal Fair by
 Alice Provensen
If I Ran the Circus by
 Dr. Suess
If I Ran the Zoo by
 Dr. Suess

Oh, Where, Oh, Where Has My Little Dog Gone?

(additional verses by Richele Bartkowiak)

Oh, where, oh, where has my
   little dog gone?
Oh, where, oh, where can he be?
With his ears cut short and his tail
   cut long,
Oh, where, oh, where can he be?

I saw him outside with his
   squeaky toy
Rolling around in the sun.
He was pouncing and bouncing
   in a pile of leaves.
Oh, it looked like jolly good fun.

I called his name six times
   or more.
I listened for his happy bark.
I looked in the shed, even by the
   back door.
I'm worried 'cause it's
   getting dark.

I looked in the garden and over
   the fence.
I even looked under two trees.
And then when I thought it was
   almost too late,
I found him asleep in
   those leaves.

Vocabulary

asleep
bark
bouncing
cut
dark
dog
fence
garden
jolly
leaves
pouncing
squeaky toy
tail

Did You Know?

○ If you lose a pet, consider the following suggestions:
   ○ Many animal shelters have "Lost and Found" bulletin boards.
   ○ Search your neighborhood. Remember to ask mail carriers and newspaper delivery people.
   ○ If allowed in your area, post signs in the neighborhood where your pet was lost.
   ○ Keep looking! Remember, many well-meaning people sometimes keep an animal, hoping to find the owner on their own.
   ○ Advertise in local newspapers and be sure to read the "Found" ads. ○ If you are fortunate enough to find your lost pet, be sure to attach a license and identification tag to his or her collar.
   ○ See page 107 for more facts about dogs.

Theme Connections

Health and Safety
Pets

Literacy Links

Comprehension
○ Ask children to use *dog* in a sentence.

Oral Language/Print Awareness
○ Encourage the children to think of names for the dog. Make a list of the names they suggest.

Phonological Awareness
○ Discuss the different types of barks dogs use. *How do they sound when they are happy to see you? How do they sound when they are angry? How do they sound when they are sad?* Ask volunteers to demonstrate.

Print Awareness
○ Print "Oh, where, oh, where has my little dog gone?" on chart paper. Point out the question mark. Ask the children if they know what it is. Tell them that a question mark at the end of a sentence means that a question is being asked.

Curriculum Connections

Discovery
○ Provide shoeboxes and materials, such as sponges, cotton, hay, twigs, and cotton batting, so the children can make miniature dog beds. *Which item will make the softest bed? Which will make the warmest bed? Will this bed be more comfortable than sleeping under the leaves?*

Fine Motor
○ Photocopy and enlarge three or four dogs from the Animal Patterns (page 113). Color them, cut them out, and laminate them. Cut the cards into puzzle pieces. Give the children the dog puzzles to work.

Special Needs Adaptation: For children with cognitive limitations, change this activity to one that focuses on teaching the concept of *large* and *small*. Copy six dogs from the animal patterns, enlarging three of them and reducing the size of three. Cut out and laminate each one. Invite the child to help you sort the dogs according to size. To make the activity more concrete, take two sheets of paper and draw a red doghouse on one and a blue doghouse on the other. Ask the child to put the small dogs in the red doghouse and the large dogs in the blue one.

Book Corner

Games

○ Hide a stuffed or plastic dog in the room and encourage children to find it. Give clues if children are old enough to follow them.

○ Give each child a photograph or magazine picture of a dog. Make sure each dog looks different. Have the children sit in a circle with their pictures. Say, "Please help me. I have lost my dog." Then describe one of the dogs. For example, you might say, "My dog has curly hair and long ears. He is a golden color." When a child realizes that she has the dog you are describing, she should say, "I can help. I have your dog. I have a golden dog with curly hair and long ears. Is this dog yours?"

Listening

○ Suggest that children practice whistling to call a dog. Demonstrate how to whistle and then encourage the children to whistle. If they are not able to whistle, suggest that they make another distinctive sound.

○ Provide a variety of dog toys. Have the children sort the items by the sound each makes. *Does it squeak? Does it rattle? Does it ring?*

Sand and Water

○ Fill the water table with leaves. If real leaves are not available, cut some out from construction paper. Provide plastic dogs for the children to hide in the leaves.

Writing

○ Provide different shapes of construction paper for the children to use to make dog tags. Help them choose a shape and then make up a name for their imaginary dogs. Print the names on the tags, if needed. Discuss lost dogs. *What can you do to make sure your lost dog finds its way back home? Is making a nametag a good idea?*

Home Connection

○ Have the children tell their family about the dog tags they made.

○ Does anyone have a dog or pet at home?

Hanky Panky

Vocabulary

banks
bullfrogs
jump

Theme Connections

Movements
Sounds

Eep! Ipe! Ope! Aap!
And a eep, ipe, ope, aap!
Down by the banks of the
Hanky Panky,
Where the bullfrogs jump
From bank to banky,
With an eep, ipe, ope, aap,
And a oops-ipsa-dilly and a
Ker-plop!

Did You Know?

o Bullfrogs are usually green to greenish-brown, and sometimes spotted. Their eyes are gold or brown, and they have a broad flat head and body. On average, they grow to be about 3 ½"–6" (9-5 cm) long in body length. Legs add another 7"-10" (17-25cm) to its length! A large bullfrog might be 16" long.

o A bullfrog has a voracious appetite and will eat anything it can fit in its mouth and swallow, even small vertebrates, such as birds, reptiles, fish, even turtles, and other frogs.

o A bullfrog can jump 20 times its length.

Literacy Links

Oral Language

o Print *bullfrog* on chart paper. Draw a line between the word *bull* and *frog*. Point out that *bullfrog* is made up of two words, *bull* and *frog*. Explain that words that are made up of two independent words are called *compound words*.

o Discuss bullfrogs. *Where do they live? What do they eat? How large do they grow? How far can they jump?*

o Teach the children the American Sign Language sign for *frog* (page 122).

Phonological Awareness

o Discuss the *onomatopoeic* words (a word that sounds like its meaning) in the song, such as *eep, ipe, oop,* and *aap. What other sounds might frogs make?*

Phonological Awareness/Letter Knowledge

❍ Print *Hanky Panky* on chart paper. Talk about how the words rhyme. Ask the children to look at the two words and point to or say which letter is different.

Curriculum Connections

Art

❍ Many bullfrogs are speckled. Provide crayons and encourage the children to make speckled pictures by dotting the crayons all over their paper.

Dramatic Play

❍ Provide plastic bugs or pictures of bugs and encourage the children to "cook" a bug stew for the bullfrogs. Be sure to provide some empty bottles of spices.

❍ Make bullfrog hats by having children glue wiggle eyes to each half of a two-inch Styrofoam ball and then gluing the Styrofoam balls to the top of a green baseball cap. Cut red felt to fit the underside of the brim and let children glue it in place. Give the children the hats and encourage them to re-enact the song.

red felt

Fine Motor

❍ Draw a frog face on a small piece of poster board. Cut a hole in the frog's mouth and glue the frog to the top of a small covered box (envelope size). Cut the hole in the mouth through the box. Provide plastic bugs and tweezers. Invite the children to use the tweezers to "feed" the frog.

> ✓ **Special Needs Adaptation:** This fine motor activity may be difficult for children with poorly developed motor skills. Adapt it by enlarging the frog face and the box to which it is attached. Try using a shoebox. Use kitchen tongs instead of tweezers, which may be too small for some children to grasp. The child can participate by feeding his giant frog.

Fine Motor/Math

❍ Spray paint the cup of a meatball press green (adult only). Glue wiggle eyes on the top of one of the cups. Place pompoms (bugs) in a bowl. Provide five paper plates with the numerals 1–5 written on the plates

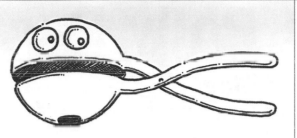

(a different number on each plate). Encourage the children to use the Frog Gobblers to pick up the correct number of bugs from the bowl and move them to the plates.

Games

○ Teach the children how to play Leap Frog. Select one child to be the frog. Have the other children get on the floor on their hands and knees and crouch down. Invite the frog to leap over the children by placing her hands on the back of each child for support while she straddles her legs around their body.

Gross Motor

○ Make two riverbanks by crumpling newspaper and covering it with a sheet. Have the children pretend to be bullfrogs jumping from bank to bank. A small bullfrog about 10" long would be able to jump 20 times it body length—that would be 16 ½' feet. *Can anyone jump that far?*

Math

○ Give the children a 10" long piece of yarn to represent a small bullfrog and a 16" long piece to represent a large bullfrog. Have the children find things in the room in both sizes. Do they find more items to match the size of a small bullfrog or large bullfrog?

 English Language Learner Strategy: Ask a child who has well-developed language skills to do this activity with an English language learner.

Writing

○ Provide Compound Word Puzzles. Print *bullfrog* on several, 4" x 12" strips of poster board. Leave a small space between *bull* and *frog*. Laminate the strips and make a puzzle cut between the two words. Encourage the children to work the Compound Word Puzzles.

Home Connection

○ Encourage the children to show their families how they can leap like frogs.

SONGS AND ACTIVITIES

Little Polly Parakeet
by Pam Schiller

(Tune: Little Bunny Foo Foo)
Little Polly Parakeet
Sits on daddy's shoulder.
When he turns his face to her,
She kisses him on the cheek.

Little Polly Parakeet
Sits on mommy's shoulder,
Whistling a happy song
Before she goes to sleep.

Little Polly Parakeet
Sits upon my shoulder.
She's soft and green and little.
She's really kinda sweet.

Vocabulary

cheek
daddy
face
green
happy
kisses
little
mommy
parakeet
shoulder
sleep
soft
song
sweet
whistling

Theme Connections

Families
Pets

Did You Know?

○ Another name for parakeets is budgies (short for Budgerigar).
○ Parakeets eat a lot of human foods. In addition to birdseed, they eat apples, carrots, lettuce, spinach, pears, raspberries, watercress, celery, alfalfa, and dandelion leaves. Just like wild birds, parakeets require more food in proportion to their size than a cat. Parakeets weigh an average of three ounces.
○ Parakeets can be yellow, green, blue, white, or gray.
○ Parakeets may enjoy sitting on your head, shoulder, or head. They enjoy human company.
○ Some parakeets talk. Almost all parakeets and parrots will mimic sounds.

Literacy Links

Oral Language
○ Talk about parakeets. Display a photo, if available. *What colors are their feathers? What do they eat? Where do they live?*
○ Teach the children the American Sign Language sign for *bird* (page 121).

Phonological Awareness

○ Print *Polly Parakeet* on chart paper. Point out the first letter of each word. Read the words. Call attention to the beginning sound of each word. Remind the children that when a sound is repeated at the beginning of several words in a phrase or a sentence it is called *alliteration*.

Print Awareness

○ Print *parakeet* on chart paper. Discuss the letters. *Which letter comes first? Which letters appear two times?*

Curriculum Connections

Fine Motor

○ Invite the children to feed the bird. Photocopy the bird from the Animal Patterns (page 119). Color it green, cut it out, and laminate it. Glue it to the lid of a small box. Use a matte knife (adult only) to cut a hole next to the bird's mouth. Give the children a cup of birdseed and tweezers. Have them use the tweezers to pick up the birdseed and "feed" the bird.

Top view

hole

bird seed

Games

○ Give each child a feather. Have them toss their feathers into the air and then try to keep the feathers aloft by blowing them up in the air.

✔ **Special Needs Adaptation:** Adapt this activity for children with limited physical skills by placing a feather on a table. Give the child a straw and ask her to move the feather by blowing through the straw. Model this for the child, so that she understands what you expect her to do. Show her each step of the activity, and ask her to repeat each step after you do it.

Gross Motor

○ Have the children walk a masking tape line with a parakeet (beanbag) on their shoulder. Have them try again with the parakeet on their head and then again with the parakeet on the back of their hand.

Book Corner

Language

○ Photocopy pages from magazines or newspapers. Enlarge the copies. Laminate them. Provide dry-erase pens and encourage the children to circle the letter "p" each time they see it.

Listening

○ Record parakeet sounds (whistles) and sentences people frequently say to parakeets, such as "Polly wants a cracker" or "Hello." Leave a space between the phrases and noises. Have the children repeat the phrases and whistles.

Music and Movement

○ Give the children two plastic or paper plates to use for wings. Play music and encourage the children to use their wings to fly to the music.

 Special Needs Adaptation: Substitute a colorful scarf for the paper plate wings. Holding the wings may be too challenging for some children with limited physical skills.

Science

○ Provide photographs or magazine pictures of parakeets. Encourage the children to find the birds' beaks, feet, wings, tails, and eyes. If at all possible, borrow a parakeet for a visit to the classroom.

Writing

○ Trace around magnetic letters to write *Polly*. Encourage the children to place the magnetic letters over the letters.

Home Connection

○ Ask families to visit a pet store where parakeets are sold.

Little Rabbit

Vocabulary

cabin
help
hopping
knock
rabbit
tired
window
woods

Theme Connections

Health and Safety
Movements

In a cabin in the woods,
Little man by his window stood.
Saw a rabbit hopping by,
Knocking at his door.
"Help me! Help me! Help
   me!" he cried!
"I'm so tired. Can I come
   inside?"
"Little rabbit come inside,
Safely to abide."

Special Needs Adaptation: Some children with special needs have great difficulty generalizing, or transferring information across objects, people, and settings. This song provides an opportunity to reinforce generalization and to expand language. A child with special needs may not understand that there are different kinds of homes, such as houses, apartments, condos, cabins, mobile homes, and so on. Bring in pictures of several types of homes and talk about each one. Invite the child to tell you about his home. Ask parents to send in a picture of the child's home, and talk about the picture with the child.

Did You Know?

o   There are 12 species of rabbits in the United States with the eastern cottontail being the most common.
o   Cottontails vary in color from gray to brown and have large ears, large hind feet, and fluffy tails. They average about a foot in length and weigh two to three pounds.
o   Rabbits live in groups in underground burrows.
o   Rabbits like to nibble on tree bark, grass, and vegetables.
o   Female rabbits can have between 20 and 40 babies a year.
o   Cottontails may live up to two years in the wild, but where predators are numerous, they seldom live more than one. Eighty-five percent of the rabbit population dies each year, including one out of every three baby rabbits born each year.

Literacy Links

Oral Language

○ Talk about feeling tired. *How does it feel to be tired? What things make you tired? What can you do to become less tired?*

○ Teach the children the American Sign Language sign for *rabbit* (page 122).

○ Discuss rabbits. *What do they eat? Where do they live? What color are they? How do they get around?*

○ Teach the children "Window Watching." *What do you think you can see out of the window?*

Window Watching
See the window I have here,
So big and wide and square. (draw a square)
I can stand in front of it,
And see the things out there. (shade eyes and look off in the distance)

Phonological Awareness

○ Encourage the children to name the rabbit in the song. Challenge them to give him a *rhyming* name such as Babbit Rabbit or Nabbit Rabbit. Then challenge them to give the rabbit an *alliterative* name like Randy Rabbit.

Curriculum Connections

Art

○ Show the children how to make circle bunnies (back view). Draw a big circle with a smaller circle sitting on top of it. Make two long ears and a little round tail.

Blocks

○ Invite the children to build a cabin. Show them how to make windows in their cabin.

Construction

○ Give each child a large brown heart and two smaller skinny brown hearts. Have the children turn their large hearts upside down and glue the skinny hearts on for ears. Invite the children to use markers to create the features for their rabbit.

Games

○ Play Go In and Out the Windows.

Go In and Out the Windows

Go in and out the windows. (IT walks around circle, weaving in and out between children)
Go in and out the windows,
Go in and out the windows,
As we have done before.

Stand and face your partner… (IT chooses a partner)
Now follow her (him) to London… (IT and partner weave through circle)
Bow before you leave her (him)… (IT leaves partner [new IT] and joins circle)

Math

○ Give the children color tiles. Challenge them to use the tiles to make square windows and rectangular windows.

Music and Movement

○ Teach the children how to do the Bunny Hop. Play bunny hop music, if possible.

Outdoors

○ Play Rabbit in the Hole. Place three hula hoops or rope circles on the ground spread out in different locations. Select one child to be the "rabbit chaser." All other children will be rabbits. Instruct the rabbit chaser to close his eyes and count to ten. The rabbits can hop into holes (hula hoops or ropes circles) any time they wish and when they are in their holes they are safe. The first rabbit tagged becomes the new rabbit chaser.

SONGS AND ACTIVITIES

Book Corner

Goodnight Moon by
　Margaret Wise
　Brown
*If You Were My
　Bunny* by Kat
　McMullan
*In a Cabin in the
　Woods* by Darcie
　McNally
My Rabbit Friend by
　Eric Rohmann
The Runaway Bunny
　by Margaret
　Wise Brown
*The Tale of Peter
　Rabbit* by Beatrix
　Potter

Snack

○ Serve "rabbit food" for snack, including lettuce, carrots, apples, and pears.

○ Invite the children to make a cottage for snack. Provide graham crackers, peanut butter, pretzels, square cereal, and small round candies. Have the children spread peanut butter on their cracker and then use the square cereal to make windows. Have them use the pretzels for a door and the candy for a doorknob. (**Allergy Warning**: Check for allergies before serving any food to children.)

Writing

○ Print *rabbit* on an index card. Provide markers and encourage the children to copy the word.

Home Connection

○ Encourage the children to look out a window at home and have a family member write down what they see. Have the children bring their stories back to school and illustrate them. Post the stories and artwork on a bulletin board entitled "Just Outside My Window."

Fido
(additional verse by Pam Schiller)

Vocabulary

dance
dog
down
front legs
hind legs
little
pup
up

Theme Connections

Circus
Pets

(Tune: Reuben, Reuben)
I have a little dog and his name is Fido.
He is nothing but a pup.
He can stand up on his hind legs
If you hold his front legs up.

I have a little dog and her name is Fifi.
She is nothing but a pup.
She can dance up on her front legs
If you hold her hind legs up.

Did You Know?

o The best way to teach a dog tricks is to make it fun and rewarding for him. Use praise and small treats to reward him. Practice new tricks only a few minutes at a time so your dog doesn't get bored when learning tricks.
o To teach a dog to shake hands, start by having him sit. Say, "Shake hands," and take his paw with your hand. Hold his paw and say, "Good dog!" Let go of his paw. Do this a few times every day.
o See pages 23 and 107 for more information about dogs.

Literacy Links

Oral Language
o Discuss pet tricks. What tricks have children seen dogs do? *Has anyone seen a dog perform at a circus or dog show?* Discuss the difference between front legs and hind legs.
o Teach the children the American Sign Language sign for *dog* (page 121).

Book Corner

Fido by Stephanie
Calmenson
Good Dog, Carl by
Alexandra Day
Pinkerton, Behave! by
Steven Kellogg

Print Awareness

❍ Print the song on chart paper. Move your hand under the words as the children sing the song. Point out the left-to-right and top-to-bottom movement of the words.

Curriculum Connections

Dramatic Play

❍ Have the children perform dog tricks for one another. Have them roll over, beg, shake, sit, and so on.

❍ Fill the center with stuffed dogs and doll clothes. Encourage the children to dress the dogs.

Gross Motor

❍ Have the children walk a balance beam. Suggest that they pretend they are a dog walking on its hind legs.

Language

❍ Photocopy the dog from the Animal Patterns (page 113) and the Rhyming Word Cards (page 120). Color the dog and Rhyming Word Cards, cut them out, and laminate them. Have the children find the items that rhyme with *dog*.

Science

❍ Provide a pulley and supervise its use as children use the pulley to pull things up and then let them back down again.

Writing

❍ Print *Fido* and *Fifi* on chart paper. Provide magnetic letters and encourage the children to use the letters copy the names.

Home Connection

❍ Ask a family to bring their dog into the classroom to show off its tricks.

The Bear Went Over the Mountain

Vocabulary

bear
mountain
other side

Theme Connections

Opposites

The bear went over the
   mountain.
The bear went over the
   mountain.
The bear went over the mountain
To see what he could see.
To see what he could see.
To see what he could see.
The bear went over the
   mountain.
The bear went over the
   mountain.

The bear went over the mountain
To see what he could see.
The other side of the mountain,
The other side of the mountain,
The other side of the mountain,
Was all that he could see.
Was all that he could see.
Was all that he could see.
The other side of the mountain,
The other side of the mountain,
The other side of the mountain
Was all that he could see!

Did You Know?

○ Brown bears live in many habitats, from desert edges to high mountain forests and ice fields. In North America, they prefer open areas, such as tundra, alpine meadows, and coastlines. Brown bears were common on the Great Plains prior to the arrival of European settlers.

○ Brown bears are one of the largest of living carnivores, ranging from 3'–7' in length from head to rump. They are 3'–5' tall at the shoulder and can tower at an intimidating height of 8' when standing upright on their hind legs. They can weigh more than 1,000 pounds.

○ Although brown bears are called carnivorous, only about 15% of what they eat is actually meat. Their diet consist of grasses, roots, berries, nuts, insects, fish, rodents, and sometimes small and large mammals.

○ See page 37 for more information on bears.

Literacy Links

Oral Language

○ Discuss *over* and *under*. Have the children think of other pairs of opposites, such as *up* and *down*, *in* and *out*, and *on* and *off*. Encourage them to demonstrate each pair.

English Language Learner Strategy: Explain that some words we use to describe things are opposites (up/down, in/out). Say, "It is not *up;* it is *down. Up* and *down* are *opposites.*" Try playing Simon Says using opposites.

Phonological Awareness

○ Discuss the growl of the grizzly bear. *What does it sound like?* Encourage volunteers to give a grizzly bear growl. Remind the children that growling is *onomatopoeia* (a word that imitates the sound it is describing).

○ Encourage the children to think of words that rhyme with bear.

Print Awareness:

○ Challenge the children to brainstorm a list of famous bears. Print the names of the bears on chart paper. How many bears did they name? Did they think of Smokey, Yogi, Winnie, Little Bear, Berenstain Bears and/or The Bear in the Big Blue House?

Curriculum Connections

Blocks

○ Provide newspaper and brown or tan sheets. Have the children crumple the newspaper and then cover the crumpled newspaper with sheets to make mountains to use in their block play.

Construction

○ Invite the children to construct bear puppets. Provide each child with a paper plate, craft stick, brown construction paper, glue, wiggle eyes, and markers. Have the children paint their plates brown to make a bear's head and then cut ears from the construction paper to glue on the bear's head. When the paint is dry, have the children glue on wiggle eyes and then use markers to make other bear facial features. Help them glue the bear head onto the craft stick to make a bear puppet. If desired, children can cut eye holes instead of using wiggle eyes and then they can hold the puppet face in front of their own face.

Field Trip

○ Visit the bears at the zoo. *How many different kinds of bears can you find?*

Fine Motor

○ Provide clay or playdough. Invite the children to shape mountains. Provide plastic bears for the children to use to move over their mountains.

○ Fold sheets of paper in half and draw half of a mountain on one side. Have the children cut along the line you have drawn and then open their paper to reveal a mountain. Point out the sameness of each side of the mountain.

Language

○ Photocopy and enlarge several bears from the Animal Patterns (page 119). Color them, cut them out, and laminate them. Glue them to craft sticks to make bear stick puppets. Have the children move their bears over tables, chairs, blocks, and so on. *Do things look different on the other side?*

Math

○ Provide symmetry mirrors (two mirrors that are hinged together). As the children draw a picture on paper, have them look in the mirror and watch what they see in the mirror.

Snack

○ Invite the children to follow the Bear Claw Rebus (page 109) to create their snack.

Home Connection

○ Have the children ask their family members to join them as they select items at home to view from two sides; for example, their bed, the kitchen table, a swing in the park, or their car. *Do the items look different when observed from different sides?*

The Bear Went Over the Mountain by Rosemary Wells

Blueberries for Sal by Robert McCloskey

Goldilocks and the Three Bears by Jan Brett

SONGS AND ACTIVITIES

Tiny Tim
(additional verses by Pam Schiller)

I had a little turtle,
His name was Tiny Tim.
I put him in the bathtub
To see if he could swim.

He drank up all the water.
He ate up all the soap.
Tiny Tim was choking
On the bubbles in his throat.

I picked up the telephone.
I pressed in 9-1-1.
I asked for the doctor
And I said he better run.

In came the doctor,
In came the nurse,
In came the lady
With the alligator purse.

They pumped out all the water.
They pumped out all the soap.
They popped the airy bubbles
As they floated from his throat.

Out went the doctor,
Out went the nurse,
Out went the lady
With the alligator purse.

Here we go again—

I had a little goldfish,
Her name was Kissy Kim.
I put her in the bathtub
To see if she could swim.

She drank up all the water.
She ate up all the soap.
Kissy Kim was choking
On the bubbles in her throat.

I picked up the telephone.
I pressed in 9-1-1.
I asked for the doctor
And I said she better run

In came the doctor,
In came the nurse,
In came the lady
With the alligator purse.

They pumped out all the water.
They pumped out all the soap.
They popped the airy bubbles
As they floated from her throat.

Out went the doctor,
Out went the nurse,
Out went the lady
With the alligator purse.

I guess we learned our lesson.
We won't try that again.
Tiny Tim and Kissy Kim
In bubbles cannot swim!

Vocabulary

alligator
bathtub
bubbles
doctor
drank
float
goldfish
lady
nurse
pump
purse
soap
swim
telephone
throat
turtle

Theme Connections

Community Workers
Health and Safety
Make-Believe

Did You Know?

○ Turtles are reptiles, and have existed more than 200 million years.

○ Turtles can live in captivity for 30–40 years.

○ The common goldfish is a type of carp, a hardy fish that has been bred and kept in ponds and aquariums for centuries in Asia. They have an average life span of about 10 years. When goldfish return to the wild, they revert to their natural colors (green to black) in just a few generations.

○ Goldfish have orange scales and long, flowing fins. The average goldfish grows to be about 3"–5" (8–13 cm) long. The largest goldfish are roughly 10" (25 cm) long.

○ Like all carp, goldfish eat tiny plants and animals by rooting in the mud on the pond floor.

○ See page 44 for more information on turtles.

Literacy Links

Comprehension

○ Ask a volunteer to move like a turtle and then to move like a fish. Talk about fish and turtles. *In what ways are they alike? How are they different?*

 English Language Learner Strategy: Show the child a photo of a turtle or a fish, and then model the corresponding movement. Have the English language learner mimic your actions. Say the name of the animal and then describe the action.

Oral Language

○ Discuss pets. *Which animals make good pets? Why? Do fish make good pets? Do turtles make good pets? Does anyone have a fish or a turtle for a pet?*

○ Teach the children the American Sign Language signs for *fish* and *turtle* (pages 122–123).

Phonological Awareness

○ Write *Tiny Tim* of a piece of chart paper. Point out the repetition of the first letter in each name. Tell the children that the repetition of the same letter sound in the first letter of each name makes this an *alliterative* name. Write *Kissy Kim* on the chart paper. Call attention to the repetition of the letter "K". Point out that this is also an *alliterative* name. Help each child turn his or her name into an *alliterative* name.

Segmentation

❍ Clap the letters in Tiny Tim and Kissy Kim. *Do the two names have the same number of letters?* Clap the syllables in each name. *Is the number of syllables in each name the same?*

Curriculum Connections

Dramatic Play

❍ Provide a stethoscope, bandages, empty pill bottles, and other materials so that the children can be a nurse or a doctor for Tiny Tim and Kissy Kim. **Note**: If you do not have a stethoscope, use an empty toilet paper tube as a stethoscope. One end is one the "patient's" chest and the other on the "doctor's" ear.

Field Trip

❍ Take a field trip to a local pet store to observe the turtles and the fish, or ask families or other classrooms that may have a turtle or a fish if their turtle or fish could visit your classroom.

Fine Motor

❍ Cut fish shapes from orange construction paper. Provide large orange sequins and glue. Invite the children to use the glue to adhere fish scales (sequins) to their fish.

Gross Motor

❍ Provide a plastic fishbowl and small plastic fish. Place a strip of masking tape on the floor to mark a throw line. Encourage the children to toss the fish into the fishbowl.

Health and Safety

❍ Teach the children how to dial 911 on the telephone. Discuss times when they might need to call for help. Stress that they must not dial 911 at any other time.

Language

❍ Photocopy and enlarge text from magazines or newspaper articles. Laminate the copies. Provide two different colors of dry-erase pens and have the children use one color to circle all the letter Ts, the first letters of Tiny Tim's name, and the other color to circle all the Ks, the first letters of Kissy Kim's name.

Fish Out of Water by
Helen Palmer
and P.D. Eastman
Yertle the Turtle by
Dr. Seuss

Math

○ Provide goldfish crackers and paper cups numbered from 1–8. Have the children count goldfish crackers into number cups and then eat them for snack.

Movement

○ Encourage the children to move like a fish. Have them swim forward and then swim backward. Invite them to crawl like a turtle. Have them roll on their backs and pull their arms and legs in to make their back arch like a turtle shell. Challenge them to rock on their "turtle shells."

Outdoors

○ Blow bubbles for the children and challenge them to think of ways to keep the bubbles aloft. Show the children how to make bubbles by blowing through their fist. Soap up your hand and then make a loose fist to act as a bubble maker. Blow through the circle made with your thumb and index finger to create big bubbles.

Sand and Water

○ Provide plastic or rubber turtles and fish for the water table and add some bubbles. Invite the children to re-enact the story.

○ See pages 45-46 for more turtle activities.

Home Connections

○ Suggest that families provide bubble baths for children and, if available, toss in a plastic or rubber turtle and fish.
○ Ask the children to talk with their families about what they have learned about when and why to call 911.

Little Skunk's Hole

(Tune: Battle Hymn of the Republic)
Oh, I stuck my head
In the little skunk's hole,
And the little skunk said,
"Well, bless my soul!
Take it out! Take it out!
Take it out! Remove it!"

Oh, I didn't take it out,
And the little skunk said,
"If you don't take it out
You'll wish you had.
Take it out! Take it out!"
Phew! I removed it!

Vocabulary

"bless my soul"
head
hole
phew
remove
skunk
stuck
wish

Theme Connections

Insects

Did You Know?
❍ Skunks are a member of the weasel family. In North America, the most common skunk is the striped skunk, which is black and identified by the white stripes running the length of its back.
❍ Striped skunks are about the size of a house cat, weighing up to ten pounds and averaging 24" in length.
❍ Skunks are most active during the late evening and early hours of the night, but are out and about during the day as well.
❍ Skunks can be found in clearings, pastures, open lands bordering forests, and on prairies. Ground burrows, old hollow logs, old buildings, board piles, junk piles, and culverts are all good places to find skunks.
❍ Skunks prefer meat but also eat plants and vegetation. They will eat insects, small animals, birds, eggs, poultry, worms, berries, grubs, and grasshoppers. Skunks are attracted to honey and foods with a strong odor.

Literacy Links

Comprehension
❍ See if the children can answer the following riddles.
  ❍ What is black and white and swims in the ocean? (whale)
  ❍ What is black and white and moos? (cow)
  ❍ What is black and white and stinks? (skunk)

Oral Language

○ Discuss the word *phew. What other words do we use to describe an unpleasant smell?* (nasty, stinky, smelly, and so on)

○ Teach the children the American Sign Language sign for *skunk* (page 122).

Phonological Awareness

○ Challenge the children to brainstorm a list of words that rhyme with skunk.

○ Have the children repeat the tongue twister, "A Skunk Sat on a Burning Stump," three times quickly. Teach them the full tongue twister:

A Skunk Sat on a Burning Stump

A skunk sat on a burning stump.
The stump thought the skunk stunk;
The skunk thought the stump stunk.

Print the tongue twister on chart paper. Underline each time the letter "s" appears. Tell the children that when a letter sound is repeated at the beginning of several words in a row it is called alliteration. Tongue twisters are alliterative.

Print Awareness

○ Have the children brainstorm a list of animals that are black and white, for example, cows, whales, seals, and panda. Write them down for the children to read back to you.

 Special Needs Adaptation: For children with cognitive challenges, add the following step to the activity. After all the children have brainstormed a list of animals that are black and white, bring in pictures of animals that are black and white and animals that are other colors. Combine the pictures, and then help them sort pictures of the animals that are black and white into one pile and the pictures of animals that are other colors into another pile.

Curriculum Connections

Art

○ Provide painting paper, paintbrushes, and black and white paint. Invite the children to paint black-and-white pictures.

Book Corner

Skunks! by David T. Greenberg

Skunks Do More Than Stink by D.M. Sousa

Discovery

○ Dip cotton balls into materials with distinctive scents, such as vinegar, vanilla extract, peppermint extract, cloves, and liquid soap. Put the scented cotton balls into separate opaque film canisters. Punch holes in the tops of the film canisters (adults only), and then cover each film canister. Ask the children to sort the scents into pleasant scents and unpleasant scents. Encourage them to identify and discuss the scents.

Math

○ Cut a hole in the bottom of a box. Provide items to try to stick through the hole, such as a book, a block, a ball, and a hat. *Which things fit and which things don't fit?*

○ Provide black and white blocks. If you don't have black and white blocks, cover blocks from the block center. Challenge the children to create black and white patterns with the blocks.

Science

○ Provide photos of animals. Have the children sort the photos into those of animals that are black and white animals and those that are not black and white.

Snack

○ Provide cream cheese, black olives, and crackers. Have the children make themselves a black-and-white snack by spreading the cream cheese on their cracker and then adding black olives on top. Yum!

Writing

○ Print *phew* on chart paper. Provide black markers and encourage the children to copy the word on white paper.

Home Connection

○ Suggest that the children tell the black-and-white riddles they learned (page 82) to their families.

Amelia's Pets

by Beverly Irby and Rafael Lara-Alecio

Vocabulary

bark	pet
bike	playful
bird	ride
cat	romp
crazy	seven
dog	silly
funny	sing
happy	sleep
hen	talk
house	turtle
parrot	walk

Theme Connections

Families
Friends
Humor

(Tune: Mary Had a Little Lamb)
Amelia has seven pets,
Seven pets, seven pets.
Amelia has seven pets
Living at her house.

Amelia has a funny parrot,
Funny parrot, funny parrot.
Amelia has a funny parrot
Talking at her house.

Amelia has a playful cat,
Playful cat, playful cat.
Amelia has a playful cat
Sleeping at her house.

Amelia has a romping dog,
Romping dog, romping dog.
Amelia has a romping dog
Barking at her house.

Amelia has a crazy turtle,
Crazy turtle, crazy turtle.
Amelia has a crazy turtle
Walking at her house.

Amelia has two happy birds,
Happy birds, happy birds.
Amelia has two happy birds
Singing at her house.

Amelia has a silly hen,
Silly hen, silly hen.
Amelia has a silly hen
Riding on a bike!

English Language Learner Strategy

Show English language learners pictures of each of the animals as they are mentioned in the song.

Did You Know?

○ There are 65 million dogs in the U.S. and 77 million cats.
○ Seventy-six million households own a pet (roughly three out of every four).
○ There are slightly more male dogs than female dogs and slightly more female cats than male cats.
○ Eighty-nine percent of pet owners believe that their pets understand all or some of what they say.
○ It's been scientifically proven that people who own pets experience less stress, have fewer heart attacks, and live longer.
○ See page 107 for more information about pets.

Literacy Links

Comprehension
❍ Read *A Bicycle for Rosaura* by Daniel Barbot. "Amelia's Pets" was inspired by this book.

Oral Language
❍ Have the children change the adjectives for the animals in the song. Explain that an adjective is used to describe something. For example, the playful cat might be changed to a sleeping cat and the romping dog might become a growling dog.
❍ Challenge the children to write a new verse for the song. You might suggest they write about a pig, a frog, a fish, or a goat.
❍ Teach the American Sign Language signs for *chicken, dog, cat, turtle*, and *bird* (pages 121-123).

Curriculum Connections

Art
❍ Encourage the children to draw their favorite pet living at Amelia's house.

Construction
❍ Read *A Bicycle for Rosaura* by Daniel Barbot. As a follow up activity, provide several junk items, such as gears, a pulley, belts, and scraps of wood. Invite the children to build something from the junk. **Note**: Use materials that fit the abilities of the children in your class. In addition, always check all materials, such as scraps of wood, to be sure that they do not pose a safety hazard.

Dramatic Play
❍ Place stuffed animals representing each of Amelia's pets in the center. Invite the children to pretend they are at Amelia's house.

Fine Motor

O Provide small boxes, wrapping paper and tape. Invite the children to wrap "presents" for the animals that live in Amelia's house.

 Special Needs Adaptation: For children with motor challenges, adapt this activity by providing larger boxes and pre-cut pieces of tape. Children can wrap larger presents for the animals. If a child has difficulty with cutting out her own paper, assist her by providing pre-cut paper.

Gross Motor

O Encourage the children to imitate the antics of Amelia's pets. For example, they can pretend to be a *romping* dog, a *walking* turtle, or a *playful* cat.

Language

O Photocopy the dog and the cat from the Animal Patterns (pages 113-119) and the Rhyming Word Cards (page 120). Color the animals and the rhyming word cards, cut them out, and laminate them. Challenge the children to find the cards that rhyme with each animal.

Math

O Provide plastic animals. Challenge the children to arrange the animals in sets of seven.

Writing

O Write the names of each of Amelia's pet on index cards. Provide tracing paper and encourage the children to trace the animal names.

Home Connection

O Have the children work with their families to determine the pets that the families have at home. Encourage them to bring to class an index card with the kind of pet written on it. Graph the responses.

Sara Sidney by Pam Schiller

(Tune: On Top of Old Smokey)
On top of a hillside (hillside)
All covered with rocks (covered
    with rocks),
There lives an iguana (iguana)
With lavender socks (with
    lavender socks).

Her name's Sara Sidney (Sidney),
Which fits her just fine (fits her
    just fine).
She has such charisma (charisma),
She's one of a kind (she's one of
    a kind).

She looks in the mirror (mirror)
And smiles a big smile (smiles a
    big smile).
I'm one great looking iguana,
    (iguana)
Just look at my style (just look at
    my style).

She bathes in the sunshine
    (sunshine)
And cools in the lake (cools in
    the lake).
She dines on tamales (tamales)

And fly-covered cake (and fly-
    covered cake).
And when she is happy (happy),
She plays her guitar (plays
    her guitar).
All the other iguanas (iguanas)
Think she's a rock star (think
    she's a rock star).

They dance on the hillside
    (hillside)
And over the rocks (over
    the rocks).
They dance with the iguana
    (iguana)
In lavender socks (in
    lavender socks).

They dance through the daylight
    (daylight)
And into the night (into the night)
Those dancing iguanas (iguanas),
A humorous sight (a humorous
    sight)!

I love that iguana (iguana),
She's really got style (really
    got style).
That silly iguana (iguana)
With the beautiful smile (with the
    beautiful smile).

Vocabulary

beautiful
cake
charisma
dance
daylight
fly-covered
guitar
happy
hillside
humorous
iguana
lake
lavender
mirror
night
one of a kind
rock star
smile
socks
style
sunshine
tamales

Theme Connections

Humor
Make-Believe

Did You Know?

❍ Iguanas can grow to be 6' long. Although the events in the song are imaginary, the subject of the song was real. Sara Sidney grew to be 52" long.

❍ Sara Sidney's original name was Sidney Schiller. Her owner thought she was a male. When the vet told her she was a female, her owner added Sara to her name. When Sara Sidney grew to be 52" long, she got a name to match her length—Sara Sidney Corinna Lovelace Schiller.

- Green iguanas like Sara Sidney live for about 15 years. Sara lived to be 11 years old.
- Iguanas usually live in trees near water. They lie on branches or on rocks beside the water. When something scares them, they jump in the water to hide.
- Iguanas eat green leafy vegetation. The will gobble a passing fly or ant, but they prefer a vegetarian diet.

Literacy Links

Oral Language

- Talk about iguanas. Discuss the difficulty of keeping an exotic animal as a pet. Make a list of easy-to-care-for pets and a list of difficult-to-care-for pets.

Phonological Awareness

- Have the children think of other words that rhyme with *rocks* and *socks*.
- Print *Sara Sidney* on chart paper. Ask a volunteer to identify the first letter in each part of the names. Say the name several times. Help children hear the repetition of the /s/ sound at the beginning of each of the names. Tell the children that the repetition of a beginning sound in a phrase or a sentence is called *alliteration*. Challenge the children to say the sentence, "Sara Sidney sings silly songs," several times quickly. Ask a volunteer to identify the repetitive sound in the sentence.

Segmentation

- Clap the syllables in Sara Sidney's first and last name. *Which part of her name has the most syllables, or do her first and last names have the same number of syllables?*

Curriculum Connections

Art

- Provide paper, paintbrushes, and lavender paint. Invite the children to paint a lavender picture.

 Special Needs Adaptation: For children with physical limitations, adapt this activity by using sponges instead of paintbrushes.

Book Corner

*The Iguana in
    Lavender Socks*
    by Pam Schiller

Construction
○ Invite the children to make shoebox guitars.
Provide empty rectangular shoeboxes or
similar small boxes and rubber bands.
Remove the lids and place rubber bands
around the bottom of the boxes. Using a
variety of widths of rubber bands creates
boxes with a range of sounds when the
rubber bands are strummed. Encourage the
children to play their guitars to songs.

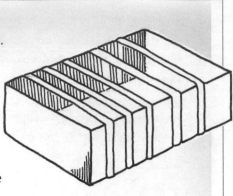

Dramatic Play
○ Provide photos of rock stars and a mirror, along with sunglasses, hats,
beads, and a variety of other costume materials. Encourage the children to
dress like a rock star.

Dramatic Play/Music
○ Ask the children to bring an old pair of white socks from home. Invite the
children to help you dye the socks lavender. **Safety note**: Closely supervise
the use of dye. When the socks dry, have the children put them on and
dance to rock music like the iguanas in lavender socks.

Fine Motor
○ Provide playdough and plastic flies (or black pipe cleaners cut into ½"
pieces to represent flies). Have the children make fly-covered cakes.

Language
○ Photocopy and enlarge text from magazines or newspaper clippings.
Laminate the copies. Provide dry-erase pens and have the children circle
each letter "s" that they can find.

Math
○ Give the children a 52" piece of yarn to represent Sara Sidney's length.
Invite them to see how many blocks they would have to place end to end
to be the same length as the yarn.

Writing
○ Invite the children to form a Sara Sidney Fan Club. Have them write fan
letters to Sara Sidney or to draw pictures of Sara Sidney.

Home Connection

○ Encourage the children to ask each family member the name of his or her
favorite rock song or rock group.

Five Little Ducks

Vocabulary

ducks
far away
five
four
hill
little
mama
one
papa
play
quack
swimming
three
two

Theme Connections

Counting
Families

Five little ducks went out one day
Over the hills and far away.
Papa duck called with a "Quack, quack, quack."
Four little ducks came swimming back.

Four little ducks went out one day
Over the hills and far away.
Papa duck called with a "Quack, quack, quack."
Three little ducks came swimming back.

Three little ducks went out one day
Over the hills and far away.
Papa duck called with a "Quack, quack, quack."
Two little ducks came swimming back.

Two little ducks went out one day
Over the hills and far away.
Papa duck called with a "Quack, quack, quack."
One little duck came swimming back.

One little duck went out one day
Over the hills and far away.
Mama duck called with a "Quack, quack, quack."
Five little ducks came swimming back.

Did You Know?

- A male duck is called a drake, a female is a duck, and a baby is a duckling.
- Ducks have webbed feet, which act like paddles. A duck waddles instead of walking because of its webbed feet.
- Ducks provide us with eggs, meat, and feathers.
- Ducks' feathers are waterproof. There is a special gland that produces oil near the tail. Ducks spread and cover the outer coat of feathers with this oil. Beneath this waterproof layer are fluffy and soft feathers to keep the duck warm.
- Ducks keep clean by preening themselves with their beaks, which they do often. They also line their nests with feathers plucked from their chest.
- Ducks make very entertaining pets. If they are raised without other ducks, they think that they are part of whatever flock they're around. Sometimes they'll believe that they're human, a chicken, or even a dog.
- See pages 33 and 107 for more information about ducks.

Literacy Links

duck

Oral Language
○ Teach the children the American Sign Language sign for *duck*.

Phonological Awareness
○ Help the children find the rhyming words in the song, such as *away/day* and *back/quack*.
○ Discuss the sound the ducks make. Explain that "quack" is an *onomatopoeic* sound, because it sounds like its meaning. Discuss other onomatopoeic sounds ducks might make. *What sound do their feet make when paddling in the water? What sound do they make when they dive? What sound do they make when they walk in the mud?*

Print Awareness
○ Print the numerals 1-5 on chart paper. Have a volunteer point to the appropriate number when it is mentioned in the song.

Curriculum Connections

Blocks
○ Provide blue paper to create a pond and rubber ducks. Encourage the children to re-enact the song.

 Special Needs Adaptation: Help children with cognitive challenges re-enact the song by providing clues to what comes next. Even if the child cannot re-enact the entire song, it may be possible for her to participate by re-enacting some part of the song.

Field Trip
○ Take a field trip to a local pond to feed the ducks. **Safety Note:** If taking the children to a water source to feed ducks, make sure to have plenty of adult volunteers and supervise children closely. Do not let them get close to the water.

Games
○ Play Duck, Duck, Goose. Children sit in a circle. One child—IT—walks around the outside of the circle, tapping each player on the head and saying "Duck." Eventually IT taps a player and says "Goose" instead. The tapped player gets up and chases IT around the circle. If she taps IT before they get around the circle, she gets to go back to her place. If she doesn't, she becomes the new IT and the game continues.

Book Corner

Gross Motor

○ Create a path of webbed footprints. Encourage the children to follow the footprints. Suggest that they rearrange the footprints and then follow the new path.

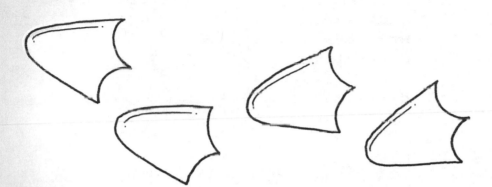

Five Little Ducks by
   Annie Kubler
*Make Way for
   Ducklings* by
   Robert
   McCloskey
The Story About Ping
   by Marjorie Flack

Music and Movement

○ Give the children white paper plates to use for wings. Play music and have the children fly like ducks.

Sand and Water

○ Provide rubber ducks for the water play table.

Science

○ Provide dried grass, small sticks, and feathers. Show the children how to build a duck nest. Explain that ducks pluck feathers from their chest to line their nests. The feathers create a soft lining that is also water repellent.

Writing

○ Print the numerals 1-5 and encourage the children to match the numerals with magnetic numbers.

○ See pages 34-35 for additional duck activities.

Home Connection

○ Encourage the children to teach the song to their families.

Fiddle-i-Fee

I had a cat,
And the cat pleased me.
Fed my cat
Under yonder tree.
Cat went fiddle-i-fee.

I had a hen,
And the hen pleased me.
Fed my hen
Under yonder tree.
Hen went chimmey-chuck,
chimmey-chuck.
Cat went fiddle-i-fee.

I had a dog,
And the dog pleased me.
Fed my dog
Under yonder tree.
Dog went bow-wow, bow-wow.
Hen went chimmey-chuck,
chimmey-chuck.
Cat went fiddle-i-fee.
Cat went fiddle-i-fee.

Vocabulary

bow-wow
cat
dog
fed
hen
pleased
tree
yonder

Theme Connections

Humor
Sounds
Things I Like

Did You Know?

○ Hens are female chickens. Roosters are male chickens.
○ The largest chicken egg on record was nearly 12 ounces, measuring 12 ¼" around. The record for a hen laying the most eggs is seven in one day.
○ There are more chickens in the world than any other domesticated bird, more than one chicken for every human on earth.
○ If a rooster is not present in a flock of hens, a hen will often take the role, stop laying eggs, and begin to crow.
○ See pages 23 and 60 for information about dogs, and page 107 for information about cats.

Literacy Links

Comprehension

○ Encourage the children to add another verse to the song. Perhaps they may want to add a duck or a pig. The sound the animals make can be completely nonsense.

Oral Language

○ Discuss *fiddle-i-fee. What does it mean? Do you think the cat is saying "thank you" or is he saying "I'm full" or something else?* Encourage the children to use their imaginations. Discuss *bow-wow* and *chimmey-chuck* in the same manner. *What do you say when you are hungry and someone feeds you?*

○ Teach the children the American Sign Language signs for *cat, dog,* and *hen (chicken)* (page 121).

Phonological Awareness

○ Discuss the sounds each animal makes. Point out the alliteration in *chimmey-chuck* and *fiddle-i-fee* and the rhyme in *bow-wow.*

cat

Curriculum Connections

Art

○ Provide tempera paint, paper, and sponges cut into the shape of a cat, a hen, and a dog (use the Animal Patterns on pages 113 and 116). Invite the children to sponge paint an animal picture.

Gross Motor

○ Draw a cat's face on poster board or make one from a paper plate. Cut out the mouth of the cat. Place the face with an open mouth on top of an empty half gallon ice cream container. Make a fishing pole by attaching a piece of yarn to the end of a cardboard tube from a coat hanger. Place a large paper clip on the other end of the yarn. Cut a fish from construction paper and hang it on the paper clip. Challenge the children to feed the cat by placing the fish on their line into the cat's mouth.

○ Draw a large dog head on the side of a medium-size box. Cut a large hole next to the dog's mouth. Turn the box so the dog head is on top. Make a throw line near the box by placing a strip of masking tape on the floor. Provide nylon or plastic dog bones (available in pet stores). Have the children toss a dog bone into the hole in the box to feed the dog.

Book Corner

Fiddle-I-Fee by
    Melissa Sweet
Play With Me by
    Marie Hall Ets

Language

○ Invite the children to dictate a sentence about things they do to "please" their families. Encourage them to illustrate their sentences.

○ Make two photocopies of the dog, the cat, and the hen from the Animal Patterns (pages 113 and 116). Color them, cut them out, and laminate them. Invite the children to play a Fiddle-i-Fee Concentration game.

 Special Needs Adaptation: For children with cognitive challenges, change this to an animal-matching activity.

Math

○ Use a permanent marker to print the numerals 1-5 on the sides of clean, empty margarine tubs. Cut a penny-size hole in the top of each tub. Make five copies of the picture of the hen from the Animal Patterns (page 116). Color them, cut them out, and laminate them. Glue one hen onto the top of each margarine tub. Provide tweezers and dried corn or unpopped popcorn. Have the children use the tweezers to pick up the corn and feed the specified number of kernels to each hen.

Music

○ Teach the children the "Whose Dog Are Thou" dance (page 106).

Outdoors

○ Play Fiddle-i-Fee chase. Select one child to be IT. Have the other children run away from IT and say, "Fee fi fiddle-i-fee, you can't catch me." The first child who is tagged becomes the next IT.

Writing

○ Print *dog*, *cat*, and *hen* on chart paper. Invite the children to use paper and crayons to copy the animal names.

Home Connection

○ Encourage the children to teach their families how to play "Fiddle-i-Fee" chase.

The Old Gray Mare

Vocabulary

ago

ain't

gray

kicked

long

many

mare

whiffletree

years

Theme Connections

Colors

Farms

The old gray mare,
She ain't what she used to be,
Ain't what she used to be,
Ain't what she used to be.
The old gray mare,
She ain't what she
Used to be
Many long years ago.
Many long years ago,
Many long years ago.
The old gray mare,
She ain't what she used to be,
Many long years ago.

The old gray mare,
She kicked on the whiffletree,
Kicked on the whiffletree,
Kicked on the whiffletree.
The old gray mare,
She kicked on the whiffletree
Many long years ago.
Many long years ago,
Many long years ago.
The old gray mare,
She kicked on the whiffletree
Many long years ago.

Did You Know?

❍ Horses belong to the *equus* family. *Equus* comes from the ancient Greek word meaning quickness.

❍ A stallion is a male horse, a mare is a female horse, and a foal is a baby horse. A pony is a fully grown small horse, not a baby horse. A young female horse is called a filly, a young male horse a colt.

❍ Horses are measured in hands. One hand is equivalent to four inches.

❍ An average life span for a horse is around 20–25 years, though they can live for up to 30 years. The oldest horse on record was "Old Billy," an English barge horse, who lived to be 62 years old.

❍ Horses love to eat short, juicy grass. They also eat hay (dried grass), especially in the winter. Extra high energy foods, such as barley, oats, maize, chaff, bran, or processed pony nuts, are good for working horses. Horses have small stomachs for their size and need to eat small amounts of food frequently. If in a field, horses will graze for most of the day.

Literacy Links

Comprehension

❍ Show children a photo of a working horse that is pulling a plow or other implement. Point out the whiffletree. (A whiffletree is a crossbar that is attached to the straps of a draft horse and to the vehicle or implement that the horse is pulling.) *Why do you think the mare kicked on the whiffletree?*

horse

Oral Language
○ Discuss the phrase "many long years ago."
○ Teach the children the American Sign Language sign for *horse*.
○ Provide a photograph of a horse. Talk about horses. Point out the mane, ears, nostrils, hooves, and tail. Make a list of what children know about horses. Make a list of things they would like to know.

> ✓ **Special Needs Adaptation:** For children who need concrete items to understand a concept, provide large plastic or stuffed horses for them to explore. It is often easier for a child to understand something if he has touched it. If possible, take the children on a field trip to see a real horse. Talk about horse safety, such as never walking behind a horse.

Print Awareness
○ Print the song on chart paper. Move your hand under the words as the children sing. Discuss the top-to-bottom and left-to-right progression of the print.

Curriculum Connections

Art
○ Provide paper, paintbrushes, and black and white paint. Encourage them to mix the paints to make the color gray and use it to paint a gray horse.

Games
○ Encourage the children to play Mare, May I? Face the children and call out to them one at a time, asking them to move toward you, making horse movements, such as galloping, trotting, loping, and walking. Encourage the children to make the sounds of a horse as they move.
○ Make a Horseshoe Game. Fill a ½–liter soda bottle with sand or pebbles to create a stake. Cut plastic coffee can lids into the U shape of horseshoes. Use masking tape to create a throw line. Invite the children to stand behind the throw line and toss the horseshoes onto the stakes.

Gross Motor

○ Remind the children what a whiffletree is (see page 97) and discuss the mare kicking at it. Place an empty wrapping paper tube between two chairs as a pretend whiffletree. Have the children stand in front of the tube and kick a leg backwards in an attempt to dislodge the "whiffletree."

Language

○ Photocopy the horse from the Animal Patterns (page 115). Make a copy for each child. Color them, cut them out, and laminate them. Cut each horse into puzzle pieces. Encourage the children to work the puzzles. Talk with the children as they work the puzzles. Discuss the way the pieces fit together. *Is it easier to match the outlines of the shapes when working the puzzles or is it easier to match the lines or colors in the puzzles?*

○ Collect several pairs of items that can be found in both old and new condition, such as books, blocks, clothes, and crayons. Have the children sort the items into new and old categories.

Math

○ Remind the children that horses are measured in hands. Give the children a four-inch piece of yarn and encourage them to find things that are one hand high. Can they find something that is two hands high or long?

Snack

○ Help the children make Haystacks for snack using the recipe on page 107. **Allergy Warning:** Check for peanut allergies.

Home Connection

○ Encourage the children to teach "The Old Gray Mare" to their family members.

Little Horse by Betsy Byars
My Pony by Susan Jeffers
The Sleep Ponies by Gudrun Ongman

SONGS AND ACTIVITIES

On the First Day of Summer

by Pam Schiller and Richele Bartkowiak

(Tune: The Twelve Days
   of Christmas)
On the first day of summer, my
   doggie brought to me—
A branch from a sycamore tree.

On the second day of summer,
   my doggie brought to me—
Two chewed-up bones
And a branch from a
   sycamore tree.

On the third day of summer, my
   doggie brought to me—
Three squeaky toys,
Two chewed-up bones,
And a branch from a
   sycamore tree.

On the fourth day of summer, my
   doggie brought to me—
Four bouncing balls,
Three squeaky toys,
Two chewed-up bones,
And a branch from a
   sycamore tree.

On the fifth day of summer, my
   doggie brought to me—
Five playful puppies,
Four bouncing balls,
Three squeaky toys,
Two chewed-up bones,
And a branch from a
   sycamore tree.

On the sixth day of summer a
   thought occurred to me—
I love the playful puppies
And the bouncing balls,
The squeaky toys and bones,
And the tree branch most of all,
But how about a special gift
   for you?

So on the sixth day of summer,
   these gifts I give to you—
Five peanut bars,
Four jerky treats,
Three old socks,
Two fluffy blankets,
And hug for my best
   friend indeed!

Vocabulary

ball
bones
bouncing
branch
chewed-up
fifth
first
fourth
playful
puppies
second
sixth
squeaky
summer
sycamore tree
third

Theme Connections

Friends
Pets
Seasons

Did You Know?

○ Dogs are social animals that crave human companionship. They thrive and behave better when living indoors with their "pack"—their human family members. This is substantiated by the experience of animal rescue volunteers and animal shelter workers as well as trainers, canine behaviorists, veterinarians, and animal welfare associations.

○ See pages 23 and 107 for more facts about dogs.

CRITTERS & COMPANY

Literacy Links

Comprehension

○ Discuss seasons. *How is summer different from other seasons? Would the doggie bring the same things home in the winter?*

Letter Knowledge

○ Print *puppy* on chart paper. Ask the children to identify the letters. *Which letter shows up three times?*

Oral Language

○ Discuss the use of the ordinal numbers, *first, second, third,* and so on. Ask the children to think of other times we use ordinal numbers. Ask volunteers to use ordinal numbers in a sentence.

○ Teach the children the American Sign Language sign for *dog* (page 121).

Curriculum Connections

Dramatic Play

○ Invite the children to pretend they are dogs in a doghouse. Provide a large box with a small door cut in one side to represent a dog house. Encourage the children to think of things a dog would want in its house. Let them decorate their house, inside and outside.

Games

○ Invite the children to play Dog and Toy as you would play Dog and Bone. Children sit in a circle. One child—IT— walks around the outside of the circle, carrying a small squeaky toy for a dog. Eventually IT drops the toy behind a player. That player picks up the toy and chases IT around the circle. If she taps IT before they get around the circle, IT goes to the "doghouse" (center of the circle). If she doesn't, IT takes her place in the circle. The player with the toy becomes the new IT and the game continues.

Book Corner

Good Dog, Carl by Alexandra Day

Harry the Dirty Dog by Gene Zion

On the First Day of Summer by Pam Schiller

The Poky Little Puppy by Jeanette Sebring Lowrey

Language

○ Photocopy the dog from the Animal Patterns (page 113) and the Rhyming Word Cards (page 120). Color the dog and Rhyming Word Cards, cut them out, and laminate them. Have the children find the items that rhyme with *dog*.

Listening

○ Provide a variety of squeaky toys. Have the children listen to the squeak of each toy and then arrange the toys from the one that makes the loudest sound to the one that makes the softest sound.

Math

○ Give the children a small branch, two dog bones, three squeaky toys, four balls, and five stuffed puppies. Have the children sequence items from least to most.

 Special Needs Adaptation: For children with cognitive challenges, adapt this activity by using fewer items to sequence. Instead of five types of items, start with two or three.

Music and Movement

○ Give the children squeaky toys to squeak to music. Call your band The Pack of Dogs Band.

Outdoors

○ Provide a box and several balls. Have the children stand back about ten feet from the box and attempt to toss a ball inside the box.

○ Encourage the children to find a partner. Provide small soft balls. One child is the dog and the other child tosses the ball to the child. Encourage the dog to retrieve the ball and bring it back to her partner. After a while, have the children switch positions.

Home Connection

○ Encourage the children to play toss and retrieve at home with a family member. Suggest that the children tell their families about the puppy in the song who kept bringing presents home to his owner.

More Learning and Fun

Songs

Little Spider Monkey
(Tune: Itsy Bitsy Spider)
The little spider monkey climbed up the banana tree
Found a banana and handed it to me.
I peeled back the skin and handed it to him
And the little spider monkey climbed up the
   tree again.

Pop! Goes the Weasel
All around the cobbler's bench
The monkey chased the weasel.
The monkey thought 'twas all in fun—
Pop! Goes the weasel.
Johnny has the whooping cough,
Mary has the measles.
That's the way the money goes—
Pop! Goes the weasel.

A penny for a spool of thread
A penny for a needle.
That's the way the money goes—
Pop! Goes the weasel.

All around the mulberry bush,
The monkey chased the weasel.
That's the way the money goes—
Pop! Goes the weasel.

Chants and Rhymes

Counting Rhyme
One, two, three, four, five,
I caught a fish alive.
Six, seven, eight, nine, ten,
I let it go again.

Five Little Mice by Pam Schiller
(Use five fingers.)
Five little grey mice running on the floor,
First one said, "What's behind the door.
Second one said, "I hope its Swiss cheese."
Third one said, "Oh, yes, cheese, please."
Fourth one said, "Where is the cat?"
Fifth one said, "Sleeping on the mat."
"Shhh," said the group,
And pitter patter went their feet
As they scampered away with a yummy cheese treat.

Five Little Monkeys
Five little monkeys jumping on the bed.
One fell off and bumped her head.
Mamma called the doctor, and the doctor said,
"No more monkeys jumping on the bed!"

(Repeat, subtracting a monkey each time. Do this
as a fingerplay or let children act it out)

I've Got a Dog
(Suit actions to words.)
I've got a dog as thin as a rail,
He's got fleas all over his tail;
Every time his tail goes flop,
The fleas on the bottom all hop to the top.

Pussycat, Pussycat

Pussycat, pussycat, where have you been?
I've been to London to visit the Queen.
Pussycat, pussycat, what did you there?
I frightened a little mouse under her chair.

Fingerplays

Five Little Fishes

Five little fishies swimming in a pool *(wiggle five fingers)*
The first one said, "The pool is cool." *(wiggle one finger)*
The second one said, "The pool is deep." *(wiggle two fingers, then point downward)*
The third one said, "I want to sleep." *(wiggle three fingers, then rest head on hands)*
The fourth one said, "Let's take a dip." *(wiggle four fingers, pretend to dive)*
The fifth one said, "I spy a ship." *(wiggle five fingers, then shade eyes)*
Fishing boat comes, *(form "V" with fingers, then move hands away from body)*
Line goes kersplash, *(pretend to throw fishing line)*
Away the five little fishies dash! *(wiggle five fingers away)*

Funny Bunny by Pam Schiller

Here comes bunny, hippety-hop *(skip finger up arm)*
See his ears, flippety-flop *(flip flop hands beside ears)*
Watch his nose, wrinkle, wrinkle, wrinkle. *(point to nose and wink)*
See his eyes, twinkle, twinkle, twinkle. *(point to eyes and blink)*
Funny little bunny, do you hear that sound? *(hand to ear as if listening)*
Is that why you hide in that hole in the ground? *(place hands over eyes as if hiding)*

Little Mousie

Here's a little mousie
Peeking through a hole. *(poke index finger of one hand through fist of the other hand)*
Peek to the left. *(wiggle finger to the left)*
Peek to the right. *(wiggle finger to the right)*
Pull your head back in, *(pull finger into fist)*
There's a cat in sight!

Five Little Mice

(Use the fingers on one hand for mice and the other hand for the cat.)
Five little mice sat down to spin;
Pussy passed by and she peeped in.
What are you doing, my little men?
Weaving coats for gentlemen.
Shall I come in and cut off your threads?
No, no, Mistress Pussy, you'd bit off our heads.
Oh, no, I'll not; I'll help you to spin.
That may be so, but you can't come in!

There Once Was a Turtle

There was a little turtle *(close hand in a fist)*
He lived in a box. *(make a box with both hands)*
He swam in a puddle, *(make swimming motions)*
He climbed on the rocks. *(use your fingers to climb up your arm)*
He snapped at a mosquito, *(clap hands)*
He snapped at a flea, *(chomp with your mouth)*
He snapped at a minnow, *(clap hands)*
He snapped at me. *(point to self)*
He caught the mosquito, *(grab air with hand)*
He caught the flea, *(grab air with hand)*
He caught the minnow, *(grab air with hand)*
But he didn't catch me. *(point to self and shake head no)*

Stories

Action Story

Monkey See, Monkey Do by Pam Schiller

(The teacher is the storyteller and the children are the monkeys. Suit your actions to words.) When my

friends and I go to the zoo, our favorite spot is the monkey house. We love to watch the funny things the monkeys do. I think perhaps the monkeys like to watch us too. I wonder if they think we are as funny as we think they are. I am never really sure exactly who is watching whom.

Hey, I have an idea. You pretend to be the monkeys, and I'll be me. I'll show you what happens at the zoo. Listen carefully, because sometimes you will be leading. Remember, you are the monkeys.

When we run up to the monkey cages, we clap our hands with glee. In no time at all, the monkeys are clapping their hands too. They jump up and down, and so do we.

We make funny faces, and so do they. They turn in circles, and so do we.

We swing our arms monkey-style (randomly all around), and they do the same.

They lift their legs up monkey-style (out to the side and up and down), and we do the same.

We scratch our heads, and they scratch their heads. They scratch under their arms, and we scratch under our arms. We pull our ears, and they pull theirs. They sit on the ground and count their toes. We pretend to do the same. Then they laugh tee-hee-hee, tee-hee-hee. That makes us roll on the ground with laughter.

Guess what the monkeys do then? You got it! They roll on the ground with laughter.

Have you ever seen the monkeys at the zoo? You really must go to see them.

When you get there, be sure to play our funny game of Monkey See, Monkey Do.

Listening Story

Tortoise Wins a Race

A tortoise named Jabotí lived in the Amazon jungle. He played a flute. All the other animals wanted his instrument, but he never gave it to anybody. One day Jabotí was walking and playing his flute. He saw Suasú, the deer.

"Hello, Jabotí," said the deer. "Where are you going?"

"Good morning," said Jabotí. "I'm going to visit my cousin."

"Where did you get that flute?" asked the deer.

"I won it in a race."

"You won it? I don't believe it!" said the deer. "You couldn't beat anyone in a race."

"You think that I am slow, but you are wrong," said Jabotí. "Do you want to race?"

"Yes," answered Suasú.

"All right. Then let's have a race!" said Jabotí.

Suasú laughed and laughed. "Do you really think you can race with me?" she asked.

"I can race with you," said Jabotí.

"Okay, let's begin right now," said the deer.

"I'm busy today," said Jabotí. "We can race tomorrow. You can run in this clearing. I know you can't run in the jungle. It is full of vines. I'll run near the edge of the jungle. When you want to know where I am, just call out and I'll answer you. Okay?"

"That is fair," answered the deer. "I have an idea, too. The winner of the race gets your flute."

Jabotí was scared. What if he lost his flute? But he couldn't say no now. "Okay," said Jabotí. He sounded brave, but he was scared. That night, Jabotí asked his family and friends to come to a meeting.

"Friends and relatives, this is a very important meeting," said Jabotí. "Tomorrow I am running a race with Suasú, the deer. I must win this race."

"That's foolish!" shouted the tortoises. "Jabotí is crazy. He can't run a race with a deer! We must do something, or he will get all of us in trouble!"

Jabotí said, "Just a minute, everybody. Let me finish." He quietly told them his plan. They all listened. The next day, Suasú came to the clearing. She was surprised to hear Jabotí's voice in the jungle.

"Good morning, my friend, Suasú. Here I am, ready to go. Are you ready?"

"Ready," answered the deer.

"One…two…three…go!" shouted the tortoise.

Suasú thought that she would win the race easily. She walked a little way. Then she looked back and called, "Jabotí!" The answer came from the jungle—ahead of her!

"Here I am. You must hurry, or I will win!"

The deer was very surprised. "How did he get ahead of me?" she asked herself. Suasú began to run. A little later, she called again. Again a voice answered from ahead of her: "Here I am, Suasú."

Suasú ran faster. But when she called again, she

heard a voice in the jungle ahead of her: "Here I am, Suasú."

So the race continued. The deer ran as fast as she could. The tortoise's voice always came from the jungle ahead of her. Finally, Suasú couldn't run anymore. She was too tired. Jabotí found her lying on the ground. Her tongue was hanging out.

"Well," said Jabotí. "A tortoise *can* win a race against a deer! You thought that you could get my flute. But look at you! You are too tired to move."

Jabotí was very happy. His plan worked. His friends and family helped him. Each tortoise took a place in the jungle, near the clearing. When Suasú called Jabotí, the tortoise ahead of her answered. Jabotí took his flute and went away. He walked and played a happy song for everyone to hear.

Note: Jabotí "won" the race because his friends and family helped him trick Suasú. Take this opportunity to talk with the children about helping others and also that it is better to win something without trickery.

Dance

Whose Dog Are Thou?

Bow, wow, wow. *(face a partner and stomp three times)*
Whose dog are thou? *(point index finger on left and right hand at partner)*
Little Farmer Tucker's dog. *(hold hands out to side)*
Bow, wow, wow. *(face partner and stomp three times)*

Games

Farmer in the Dell
(Choose one child to be the farmer. The other children walk in a circle around the farmer. Sing the song together.)

The farmer in the dell, the farmer in the dell.
Hi-ho the derry-o, the farmer in the dell.

The farmer takes a wife (husband or friend)
   (farmer brings a second child into the circle)
The farmer takes a (husband or friend).
Hi-ho the derry-o, the farmer takes a wife
   (husband or friend).

The wife (husband or friend) takes a child. *(wife chooses a third child to join in the circle)*
The child takes a dog…
The dog takes a cat…
The cat takes a rat…
The rat takes the cheese…

The cheese stands alone… *(everyone except cheese leaves the center of the circle)*

Old Gray Cat

The old gray cat is sleeping, sleeping, sleeping.
The old gray cat is sleeping in the house.
(one child is cat and curls up, pretending to sleep)

The little mice are creeping, creeping, creeping.
The little mice are creeping through the house.
(other children are mice creeping around sleeping cat)

The old gray cat is waking, waking, waking.
The old gray cat is waking through the house.
(cat slowly sits up and stretches)

The old gray cat is chasing, chasing, chasing.
The old gray cat is chasing through the house.
(cat chases mice)

All the mice are squealing, squealing, squealing.
All the mice are squealing through the house.
(mice squeal; when cat catches a mouse, that mouse becomes the cat)

Interesting Critters and Company Facts

Bullfrogs
- Female bullfrogs have eardrums the same size as their eyes. The male bullfrog has a larger eardrum.
- Bullfrogs are native to the eastern United States, ranging from as far north as Nova Scotia, all the way down to central Florida. They also live as far west as Wisconsin and the Rockies.

Cats
- In the animal kingdom, the IQ of a cat is surpassed only by that of monkeys and chimps.
- Cats purr at about 26 cycles per second, which is similar to the frequency of an idling diesel engine.
- Cats sleep about 16 hours a day, which is more than virtually any other animal.

Dogs
- When Pompeii—the Roman community destroyed by Mount Vesuvius in AD 79—was excavated, searchers found evidence of a dog lying across a child, apparently trying to protect the youngster.
- Mosaics meaning "Beware the Dog" were found on doorsteps in ancient Roman cities.

Ducks
- Ducks were domesticated by the Chinese many hundreds of years ago.
- Ducks' feet have no nerves or blood vessels. This means ducks never feel the cold, even if they swim in icy cold water.

Elephants
- Elephants are the largest mammals in the world that live on land.
- There are two kinds of elephants: African and Asian. Asian elephants have smaller ears and shorter tusks than African elephants. The African elephant is larger and taller than the Asian elephant. Elephants can live as long as eighty years!
- Elephants never stop growing throughout their lifetime and, thus, size is a good indicator of age—the larger the elephant, the older he or she is.
- Elephants live in families. Several families live together in a herd. The leader of the herd is usually the oldest female elephant. She is called the *matriarch*. All the babies and other females follow her. A young male elephant stays with the herd until he is fourteen or fifteen years old and then goes out on his own to find a female elephant for a companion.
- An elephant's trunk is part nose and part upper lip. Elephants can breathe through their trunks. They can also smell and pick things up with it. They use it to put food into their mouths, and can even spray water with it! The trunk is used to feel things, too! Baby elephants often insert their trunks into their mouths and suck on them—much like a human child sucks on its thumbs.

Recipe

Haystacks
12 ounces butterscotch morsels
6 ½-ounce can of peanuts
5-ounce can of Chow Mein noodles
saucepan
stove or hot plate
wax paper

Melt the butterscotch morsels over medium heat (adult only). Stir in the peanuts and the Chow Mein noodles. Spoon onto wax paper. When cool enough to handle, the children can shape them into haystacks. **Allergy Warning:** Check for peanut allergies.

Animal Ice Cream Rebus

Animal Ice Cream Recipe

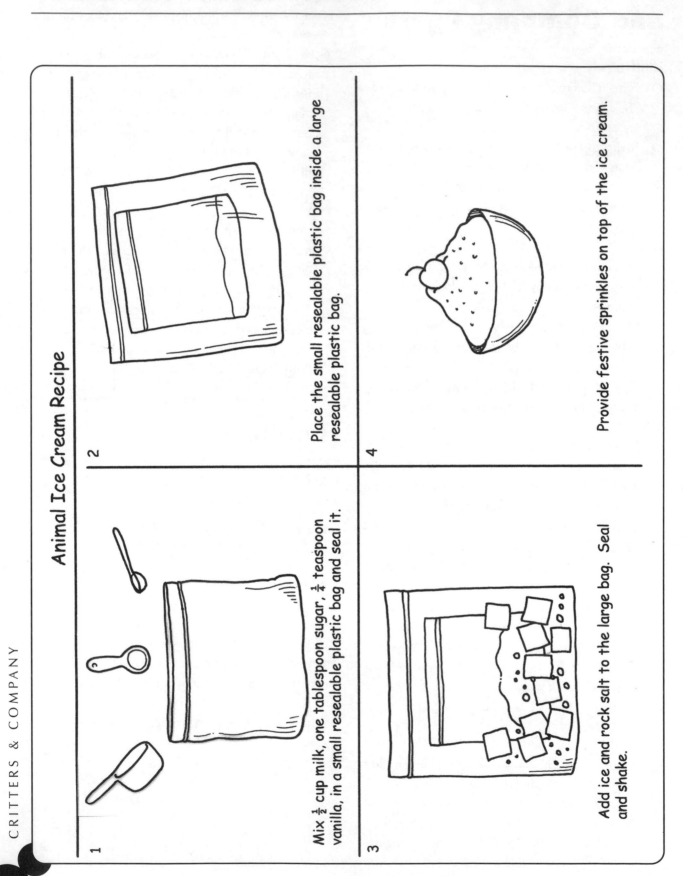

1 Mix ½ cup milk, one tablespoon sugar, ¼ teaspoon vanilla, in a small resealable plastic bag and seal it.

2 Place the small resealable plastic bag inside a large resealable plastic bag.

3 Add ice and rock salt to the large bag. Seal and shake.

4 Provide festive sprinkles on top of the ice cream.

Bear Claw Rebus

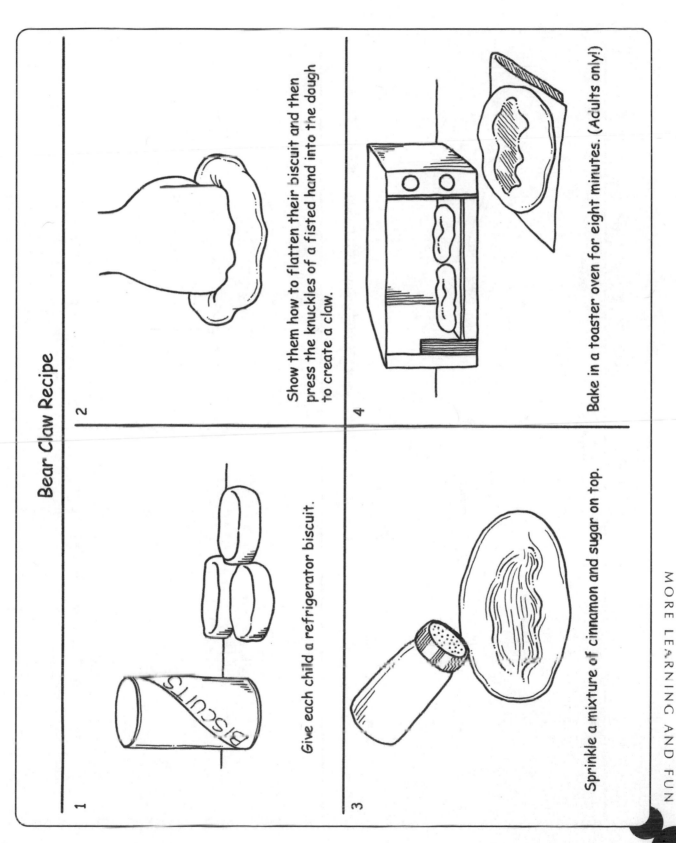

Bear Claw Recipe

1. Give each child a refrigerator biscuit.

2. Show them how to flatten their biscuit and then press the knuckles of a fisted hand into the dough to create a claw.

3. Sprinkle a mixture of cinnamon and sugar on top.

4. Bake in a toaster oven for eight minutes. (Adults only!)

Friendly Spider Rebus Recipes

Friendly Spider Recipe (peanut butter allergy alert!)

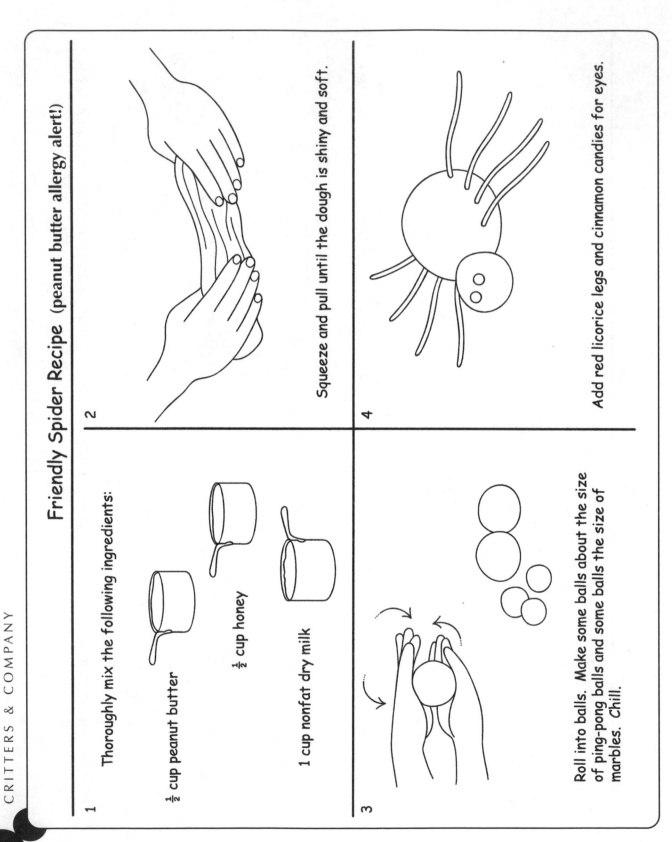

1 Thoroughly mix the following ingredients:

$\frac{1}{2}$ cup peanut butter

$\frac{1}{2}$ cup honey

1 cup nonfat dry milk

2 Squeeze and pull until the dough is shiny and soft.

3 Roll into balls. Make some balls about the size of ping-pong balls and some balls the size of marbles. Chill.

4 Add red licorice legs and cinnamon candies for eyes.

Mice Ice Cream Rebus Recipe

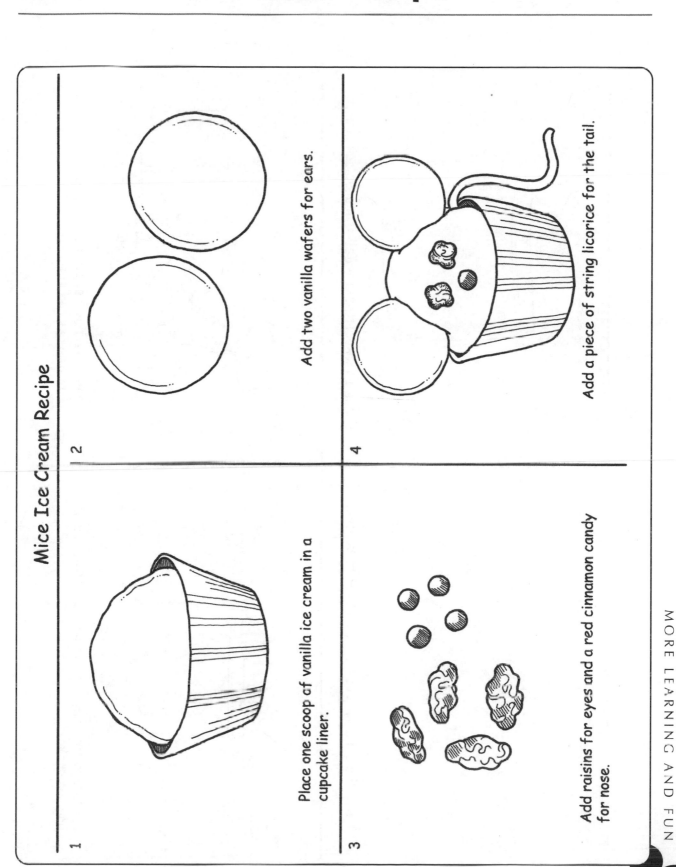

Mice Ice Cream Recipe

1

Place one scoop of vanilla ice cream in a cupcake liner.

2

Add two vanilla wafers for ears.

3

Add raisins for eyes and a red cinnamon candy for nose.

4

Add a piece of string licorice for the tail.

Monkey Treat Rebus Recipe

Monkey Treat

Place 1 teaspoon of dry Jell-O®in a ziplock bag.

Remove the bicycle banana wheels with toothpicks and eat.

Give the children plastic knives to slice bananas.

Encourage children to put 3 or 4 banana slices in bag and shake.

Animal Patterns

Animal Patterns

Animal Patterns

Animal Patterns

Animal Patterns

Animal Patterns

Animal Patterns

hat

bat

log

hog

house

hair

stair

American Sign Language Signs

bear

bird

cat

chicken/hen

dog

donkey

duck

elephant

American Sign Language Signs

fish

frog

horse

I love you

mouse/mice

monkey

rabbit

skunk

American Sign Language Signs

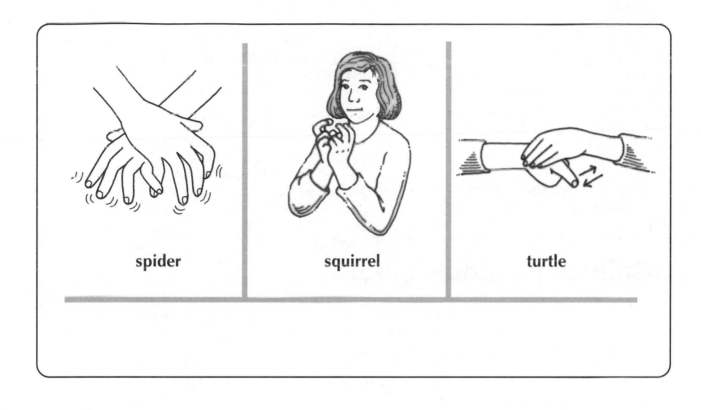

spider   squirrel   turtle

References and Bibliography

Bulloch, K. 2003. *The mystery of modifying: Creative solutions*. Huntsville, TX: Education Service Center, Region VI.

Cavallaro, C. & M. Haney. 1999. *Preschool inclusion*. Baltimore, MD: Paul H. Brookes Publishing Company.

Gray, T. and S. Fleischman. Dec. 2004-Jan. 2005. "Research matters: Successful strategies for English language learners." *Educational Leadership*, 62, 84-85.

Hanniford, C. 1995. *Smart moves: Why learning is not all in your head*. Arlington, VA: Great Ocean Publications, p. 146.

Keller, M. 2004. "Warm weather boosts mood, broadens the mind." Post Doctoral Study: The University of Michigan, Anne Arbor, MI.

LeDoux, J. 1993. "Emotional memory systems in the brain." *Behavioral and Brain Research*, 58.

Theme Index

Children's Book Index

Index